"THIS EDIFICE IS COLOSSAL": 19TH-CENTURY ARCHITECTURAL PHOTOGRAPHY

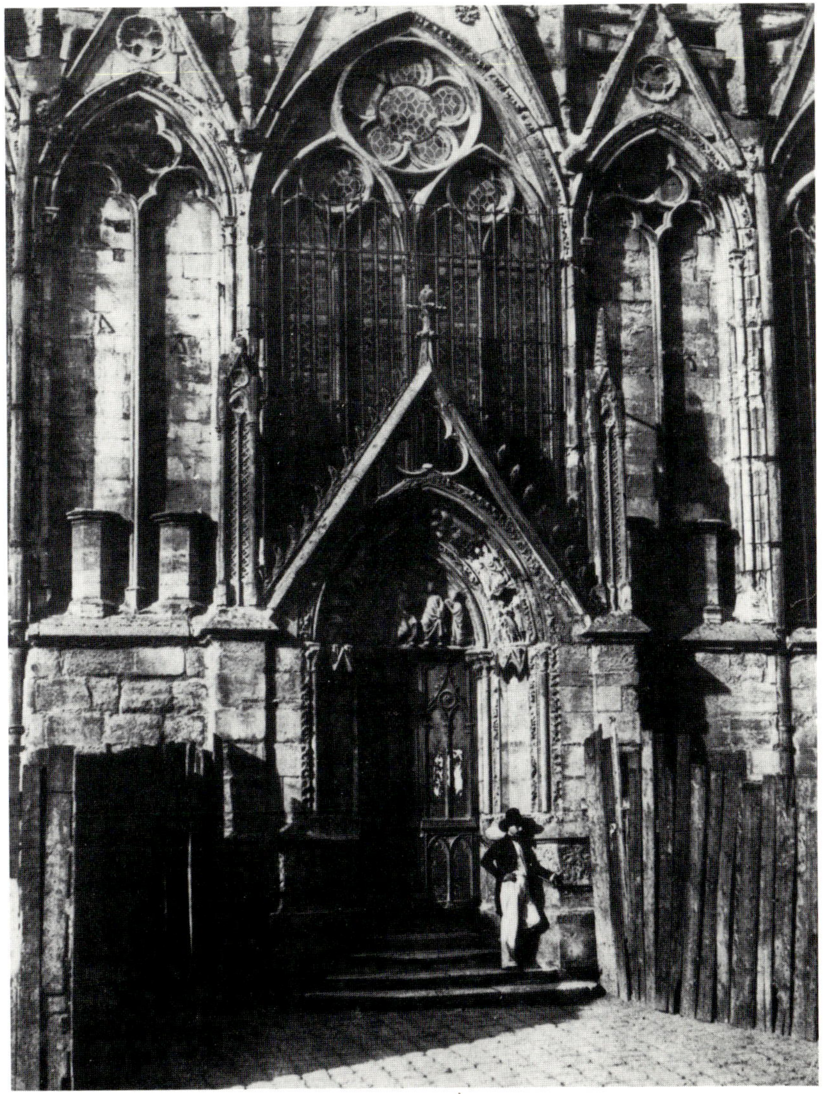

ROBERT A. SOBIESZEK

International Museum of Photography at George Eastman House

For the past century and a half, an enormous record of world architecture has been created by photographers, a colossal edifice of images, as it were, that documents and interprets the noblest constructions of mankind, the architect's most inspired expressions, and the social fabric of building that surrounds us.

Since its beginnings in the early 19th century, photography has had a special relationship with architecture. Indeed, the earliest examples of the art of photography are of architecture, quite simply because buildings were interesting subjects and because their stationary qualities were perfectly suited to the lengthy exposure times then required. Within months of the public announcement of photography's invention in August 1839, photographers focused their new equipment on the great architectural monuments of the past and present. And within only a few years the profession of architectural photography was firmly established, as were the vast majority of techniques and skills required to meaningfully translate an edifice into a picture. Most of these techniques are still in use today, the earliest tricks have become conventions, and the finest of these photographs have endured as standards against which to judge more recent achievements.

Photographs of architecture were made by various kinds of camera artists during the last century and served a wide range of purposes. Early explorers took cameras with them to record the marvels they encountered, governments commissioned photographers to survey the principal relics of their past. Architects discovered photographs as unprecedented source material for their designs and began to find photographs of their buildings useful as personal histories and as tools for self-promotion. City planners hired photographers to verify the deterioration that existed before and the progressive benefits that came after urbanization.

Engineers had photographs taken in order to study construction techniques. Last but not least, everyday people took photographs of their homes for the simple pleasures of honoring what was important to them.

In 1857, the Architectural Photographic Association was founded and held its first meeting at the Institute of British Architects. Its objectives were "the procuring and supplying to its members photographs of architectural works of all countries," and its benefits would be "to the architectural profession by obtaining absolutely correct representations of these works, and, to the public, by diffusing a knowledge of the best examples of architecture, and thereby promoting an increased interest and love of the art."[1] Before the 1880s, commercial photographers established studios in critical locations around the world, selling souvenir photographs of sites and monuments to European and American travelers; after the introduction of the hand-held camera simplified picture taking, countless tourists captured their own memories of these same sites and monuments. Whether professional or amateur, whether taken by a large view camera or a folding Kodak, these images furnish us with an invaluable testament to architectural facts and attitudes at the beginning of our modern era.

19th-century architectural photographs, however, are much more than just wonderful pictures of great and interesting buildings. They are about history—not just the history of the architecture that was being captured on film, but the history of the last century as well. While these images document architecture, they also reflect their period's tastes in art and style, they follow national paths of expansion and colonialism, they exhibit the past century's fascination with archaeology and ancient cultures, they chart the rise of Western travel and tourism, and they measure in good part the tremendous changes that occurred at this time in the name of progress. It was a period of historicisms and new technologies; of Greek, Egyptian, and Gothic revivals; of modern steel and glass constructions and suspension bridges; of urban squalor and urban renewals; of classical imperialism and picturesque romanticism.

Of the countless architectural photographs made roughly between 1839 and 1900, two in particular seem to summarize the principle motivations behind photographing buildings during the last century. Both of these images appeared in 1856 in the pages of the first, truly great, architectural journal, the *Revue générale de l'architecture et des travaux publics*. Founded and edited by César Daly, the journal was, for nearly a half-century between 1840 and 1889, "one of the few architectural journals to develop and defend a coherent architectural philosophy which, while influenced by and affiliated with the work of a group of contemporary architects, was independent of any traditional or self-declared school."[2]

As early as 1851, César Daly had joined in two meetings of the Société héliographique, along with the photographers Gustave Le Gray, Eugène Piot, and Hippolyte Bayard, to discuss whether illustrating the *Revue générale* with photographic prints was feasible.[3] Most of the discussion centered around each photographer's estimate of the high costs involved and various production problems. At the second session, a letter from the photographer Louis-Désiré Blanquart-Evrard was read in which he proposed a photographic printing firm in Lille that would accommodate up to 6,000 prints per day at a cost even Mr. Daly could afford. Between 1852 and 1856, Blanquart-Evrard printed for and published a number of excellent, photographically illustrated books, albums, and portfolios; but no journal or periodical, not even the premier photographic journal *La Lumière*, took him up on his offer of 1851. Thus, in 1856 and with these two photographs,

Daly finally tested the economics of various types of photographic illustration, none of which were ever adopted on a regular basis in the *Revue générale*. Yet in terms of what they signify architecturally and what they reveal photographically, these two very different prints mark the extremes of both architecture and its photography during the last century.

The first is an actual photographic print on albumen paper depicting the famed spiral staircase located in the François I wing of the Chateau de Blois (cat. 47). The second image is a photolithograph by the Poitevin process representing the iron framework of the celebrated Halles Centrales, or central market, in Paris during its construction (cat. 104).

The photograph of the staircase was the first photographic illustration to be published in the journal, appearing as plate 21 in volume XIV (1856). The photographer is unidentified, but it seems reasonable to attribute the print to François-Alphonse Fortier (died 1882). The Chateau de Blois was completed in 1508 and its centerpiece, this "corkscrew" staircase, was believed during the 19th-century to have been designed by Leonardo da Vinci, although there is no real evidence to that effect. The Chateau had been completely restored in 1847 by Félix-Jacques Duban (1797-1870), the principal architect of the Ecole des Beaux-Arts building in Paris during the 1830s. Commenting about the print and the Chateau, the architect Henry Sirodot wrote:

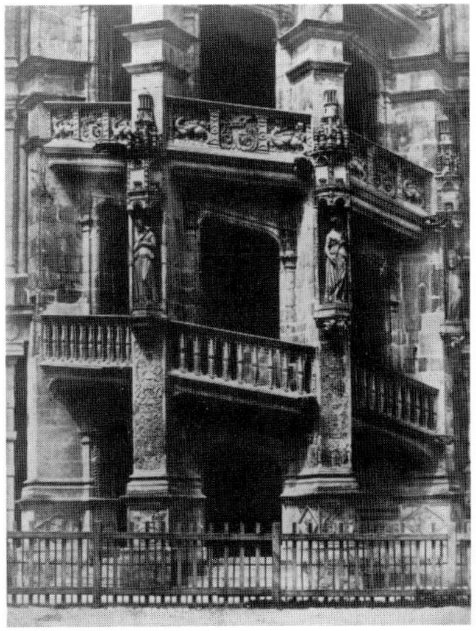

47

Plate XXI, an example of the resources that representing monuments by collodion offers us, shows the lower part of the staircase of the Chateau de Blois—that charming creation of the most flourishing part of the Renaissance—which had been abandoned, mutilated, and fallen into ruin, and has been recently given a new attire by the magic wand of the grand magician, Mr. Duban. [4]

The photograph did not simply document a notable monument from French architectural history. It also celebrated a contemporary achievement: that monument's restoration and, thus, the Second Empire's meritorious attitude towards the conservation of its own past. Although Baron Georges-Eugène Haussmann was at the same time leveling entire sections of historic Paris in line with his modernization of the city's plan, the same government that hired him also sponsored numerous architectural restorations as well as the Commission des monuments historiques.

The Chateau de Blois was classical French Renaissance, constructed out of solid, impenetrable masonry, and with an aura of genius and romance attached to it. The architect who directed the restoration of it was Beaux-Arts trained, socially and politically well-connected, and a talented traditionalist. Whoever the photographer might have been, he would have had at least a general understanding of these facts and would have made certain choices in light of them in his interpretation of the building. The staircase is evenly lighted in order to obtain a detailed record of the masonry and the carved decoration. Not even the deepest shadows seem very obscure. To achieve this effect, both the time of day and the weather had to be taken into account. Unquestionably, the day was overcast, which would allow for such an even, soft light, and the brightest part of the sky was behind the photographer, thereby filling in the deeper parts of the staircase.

More significant, however, was the photographer's choice of vantage point. He might have photographed the stairway from an oblique angle or from further away, thereby portraying more of the edifice. Instead, he chose to take a close-up view immediately in front of the staircase. In this way, he not only monumentalized his subject by having it nearly fill the image, but he also linked his photograph to the dominant, Beaux-Arts style of rendering grand architecture in drawing: the frontal view of the principal elevation—perspectiveless, imperial, with little or no extraneous details around the edifice, and isolated from its broader context. By monumentalizing the staircase, the photographer conveyed a certain amount of grandeur to the building and importance to its restoration. By treating it in the style of an elevational rendering, he conformed to an established pictorial vocabulary that was legible to every architect and the public. This fashion of architectural photography, what we might call the photography of the imperial façade, soon reached its most masterful expression in the work of such photographers as Edouard-Denis Baldus, the Bisson brothers, Robert Macpherson, and the Alinaris. And what had become a pictorial convention during the 1850s, still obtains today in the photography of most corporate headquarters and government buildings.

Such images, wrote Sirodot in the text to this image, "have become a source of study that utterly and completely satisfies our epoque's need for precision." Yet, and here we sense this architect's uncertainty before the first photograph published in his profession's journal, he hesitated in fully accepting the camera's portrayal of architecture: "in spite of the admirable fidelity of the numerous details presented in the print, the spirit is not satisfied.... As marvelous as the instrument of photography might be, there is still another that is even more marvelous, one which nature has so liberally provided us and which we take nearly for granted: the human eye."[5] This same architect and critic also called Joseph Paxton's great Crystal Palace of 1851 "no more than a giant greenhouse, without pretensions to architecture."[6] Of equal interest, however, early published photographs of the Chateau de Blois contributed chiefly to the "chateauesque" element in American domestic architecture, such as Richard Morris Hunt's "Biltmore," the Vanderbilt estate near Asheville, North Carolina.[7]

The second photograph, that of the Halles Centrales in Paris, appeared in the same volume of the *Revue générale* as plate 41, and was also accompanied by a short text by Sirodot. Here, Sirodot made no further comment about photography, except that "the photographic view has been reproduced by the lithographic process discovered by Mr. Poitevin."[8] In his essay accompanying the Chateau de Blois photograph two months earlier, Sirodot promised that the next photographic illustration was to be in the form of a photolithograph instead of a silver print, and that this was in part an experiment by the journal to determine the practicality of such illustrations.

The Halles Centrales of Paris were designed by Victor Baltard (1805-1874) and Félix-Emmanuel Callet (1792-1854) and were that city's first great iron-work construction. They were built between 1853 and 1857, following Joseph Paxton's

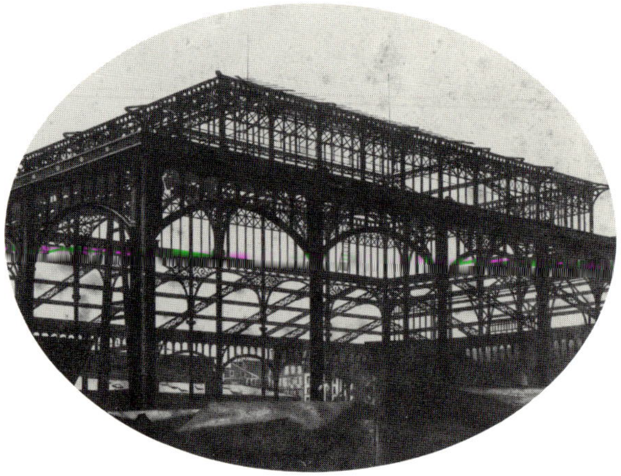

104

revolutionary Crystal Palace of 1851 in London and contemporary with the even vaster Hall of Machines at the Exposition universelle of 1855 in Paris. Writing about the photograph, Sirodot commented:

The hall or, to use the term consecrated by usage, the Central Halls are composed not of isolated constructions . . . but of eight pavilions linked together by covered streets, as if forming a vast cover under which all the merchandise is spread out which used to be distributed in so many separate markets. Plate XLI offers us a view of the Southwestern pavilion during its construction; it is of a stage of the construction, taken at the most interesting moment of assembling the pieces, revealing the disposition of the framework.[9]

Thematically, it is interesting that Daly chose this image for the *Revue générale*. Where the Chateau de Blois photograph depicted an historical edifice, solidly rooted in traditional forms and construction methods, here we are confronted with a building that is so new it is still under construction and entirely modern in its shapes and use of materials. Where the first image looked to the past and its preservation, this one looks to the future, renewal, and progress. Where the earlier print represented an edifice built by an "architect" and restored by yet another, this print shows a construction that was closer to engineering than architecture. During the 1850s, the debate between architects and engineers, between the traditionalists and the modernists, between the Ecole des Beaux-Arts and the Ecole Polytechnique, raged heatedly. In the long run, of course, the modernists prevailed. In 1869, Jean-Louis-Charles Garnier (1825-1898), the architect of the quintessential Beaux-Arts monument of the last century, the Paris Opera, wrote

The distinction between architect and engineer is a rather modern one. It takes a portion of a whole and makes it a speciality; it divides an art into two parts, and one of them it makes a distinct profession. . . . This is an irrationality that cannot be explained, a strange misinterpretation of the art of building. Who can really demarcate? Where does art begin? Where does it end? The bridge, the viaduct, even the roundhouse can be as artistic as the railway terminal, and architecture can be manifested in a cabin as well as a palace.[10]

By illustrating Baltard's Halles Centrales, the *Revue générale* not only presented another form of photographic illustration, but in essence also validated the opposing side of the architectural debate then in progress.

Photographically, too, the image is distinctly different from the earlier one. Instead of a direct, frontal confrontation with the edifice, the unknown photographer —perhaps Alphonse Poitevin

(1819-1882) who printed the lithograph—tilted his camera upwards towards the corner of the structure, thereby recording a two-point perspective view which placed the building solidly in its own space. While perspective renderings were part of any trained architect's vocabulary, they were seldom, outside of America, professionally treated with the seriousness accorded drawings of the building's plan, cross-sections, and elevations. Compared to the majority of engraved illustrations in the *Revue générale*, perspective views were clearly the exception. Again, instead of choosing an even lighting that would flatten the surface features of the edifice and by not positioning the camera in or atop a surrounding building for a higher vantage point, the photographer silhouetted the construction against a much lighter sky. In doing so, the delicate and complicated iron traceries of the Halles Centrales are forcefully dramatized as well as documented. The picture is, in spite of the modernism of the architecture, also rather picturesque. Construction materials are scattered across the foreground, parts of the urban context are seen through the open framework, and the stucture seems to grow almost organically from the dark ground, looming before us on the verge of a new era.

The picturesque style in architectural photography—that style which emphasized the perspectival and the contextual—was more popular with British and American, rather than French, photographers. Based in the traditions of watercolor painting, travel illustrations, and visionary scenics, perspective views were championed by such photographers as Francis Frith, Samuel Bourne, Timothy O'Sullivan, and Frederick Evans.

Together, the two photographs illuminate the modalities of 19th-century architecture. The one speaks about a domestic chateau in the country, classical traditions, archaeology and history, and the responsibilities pertaining to cultural heritage. The other speaks about a commercial marketplace in the center of a swiftly changing metropolis, modern forms with new materials, sociology and engineering, and faith in technological progress.

The two images also signify the modalities of 19th-century architectural photography and, by extension, all architectural photography. From its beginnings, the photography of architecture was concerned with recording the past, thus preserving it; and with documenting the present, thereby collecting evidences of future trends. The frontal portrayal of monuments isolated from their larger context is as much a consideration of style and intention as the more picturesque, perspective view of architecture surrounded by the accidents of its environment. From his travels in the Loire valley, the photographer of the Chateau de Blois brought back a document, like a photograph of any foreign monument, with which "one could enjoy the spectacles or devote oneself to studies that until then had been the exclusive privilege of a few happy travelers—it is the world in a portfolio or, to use Alfred de Musset's expression, the spectacle in an armchair."[11] From his daily experience within the ever-changing urban panorama, the cameraman of the Halles Centrales not only captured an instructive moment during a monument's construction, but also pictured what the poet Théophile Gautier meant when he said, "mankind will produce a completely new architecture out of its period exactly at the moment when the new methods created by recently born industry are made use of."[12]

Problems of distribution and publication of architectural photography are also at issue with these two prints. One is an actual photograph, the other a photomechanical reproduction of a photograph. Where silver prints are completely unparalleled in their detail and tonal richness, they are severely limited by the costs and labor involved in using them as illustrations to books or periodicals. Furthermore, many early photographic processes tended to fade, even when bound and secured between covers. From the first engravings or lithographs hand-copied from photographs, architectural photography began developing towards those photomechanical means—photogravure, collotype prints, half-tone engravings, etc.—that would, later in the century, disseminate the image of architecture to an ever-increasing audience. Only in this century, however, was this goal really achieved with the advent of photo-illustrated architectural magazines during the 1920s and 1930s. Yet, both photographically and photo-mechanically, what went before, during the last century, has never been surpassed in photographic quality or in interpretive vision.

With these two prints in mind, the present exhibition has been structured and arranged into six sections, following the principal thematic concerns of architectural photography during the last century. In "Antiquity and Archaeology," the issue is the antiquarian vision of the ancient past, as well as the "past" of primitive and exotic cultures, such as those of the Far East, Latin America, and native North America. Included are prints that were made as much for the archaeologist and anthropologist as they might have been for the architectural historian or the adventuresome traveler. The "spectacle in the armchair" is most appropriately descriptive of the work in this section.

In "European History," it is the more immediate presence, both historiographic and touristic, of a European past, extending from the Middle Ages to the late 18th century, that is of primary significance. The work of early national surveys, such as the Mission des monuments historiques in France, and that of the great "view" or *vedutti* photographers of Italy and elsewhere are examined here. With much of Europe's architectural heritage threatened by centuries of neglect and by urban expansion, the role of the photographer was literally that of a pictorial preservationist. And with increased tourist demand for mementoes of the Grand Tour, photographers found a steady clientele for pictures of Europe's greatest historical sites.

19th-century attitudes towards its own building styles are examined in the section entitled "Contemporary Architectural Expressions." From the construction of the Sir Walter Scott monument in Edinburgh to a country church with a "Doric" façade somewhere in France, from Robert Mills's U.S. Treasury Building in Washington to an Art-Nouveau shopfront in Paris, the photographer helped celebrate the latest in traditional, revivalist, and avant-garde architecture.

The images in "The Rustic and the Vernacular" have been chosen to reflect the same period's fascination with picturesque, rural life and its primitive architecture, as well as with the quaint architecture of the suburbs. Realist and naturalist art of the mid-century brought with it an increased fascination in country living and manners. The growth of modern cities saw the development of new communities, the suburbs, with their own particular life styles and their own architectures—communities that were in turn depicted by the Impressionists. Of parallel interest in this country, was the romance of the frontier and its new settlements.

"**P**rogress and Construction" focuses on the new methods of construction and building that were progressively a part of architecture during the last half of the century. From Joseph Paxton's early greenhouse at Chatsworth to Charles Garnier's Paris Opera, from the masterpieces of marine architecture to the latest factories, the art of building and our ways of judging architecture changed dramatically during the last century. With this kind of architecture, the photographer was just as likely to be in the service of the general contractor or the engineer as he would have been to the architect or general public.

Finally, the portrayal of the city, an important subject for photography during an age which witnessed the origins of the modern urban complex and urban renewal, is presented in the section "Old Cities and New." Sensing that the machinery of urbanization, whether in Glasgow, Paris, Hamburg, or Vienna, would soon eradicate much that was squalid and unhealthy but also of considerable historic interest, architectural societies, municipal governments, and individual photographers sought to document what they could before it disappeared. While a few American cities were beginning to wrestle with similar problems, the general mood in this country was more positive and expansive, especially when confronted with the newest of cities and the latest towns spawned by the railway. It was in the city, too, that photography's singular capacity for stopping action in mid-stride found a perfect expression of the early modern era.

Architecture is unquestionably the greatest and the most ubiquitous of the arts. Photographs of it, while never intending to be substitutes for direct experience, allow us to read much of what architecture expresses, since all building is a social and cultural text by its very nature. In what is undeniably the greatest 19th-century novel about architecture—Victor Hugo's *Notre Dame of Paris* published in 1831—the archdeacon Claude Frollo points to Notre-Dame and asserts that it is one of his books. The great monuments of past architecture, for Hugo, were constructed to reveal both faith and knowledge. In the Paris of 1482, Dom Claude knew how to read the text of the cathedral, but at the same time feared that Guttenberg's invention of moveable type and the advent of printed books would usurp this traditional role of architecture. Looking from a printed book to the church, he says "Alas, this will kill that . . . the book will kill the building."[13] Later in the novel, Hugo explains that the accumulation of printed texts since the 15th century was in fact itself an immense architecture which, like the Gothic cathedral, informed the public on matters of theology, science, and art. When he states that "this edifice is colossal," he refers not to architecture but to literature, a colossal edifice of knowledge and information.

Up to Hugo's time, all knowledge and information about historical or contemporary architecture was communicated through the written word and often less than accurate, hand-drawn images. After 1839, photographers began constructing yet another colossal edifice, this time built from photographs instead of words. By 1900, every known architectural masterpiece, every ancient monument, every city, and examples of most vernacular styles of building had been photographed. Many of the sites photographed in the last century exist today only in these images. Deterioration, wars, renovations, urbanization, and disasters, both man-made and natural, have taken their toll of our architectural heritage. Out of the vast archives of photographic imagery, we can savor this heritage and read the text of architectural history in a manner that is both instructive and, at its best, brilliantly spectacular.

Robert A. Sobieszek

NOTES

[1] *Builder,* XV (1857), p. 249.

[2] Ann Lorenz Van Zanten, "Form and Society: César Daly and the Revue Générale de l'Architecture," *Oppositions,* 8 (Spring 1977), p. 137.

[3] See F. A. Renard and Duveaux, "Société héliographique. Séance du 21 mars 1851 . . . ," *La Lumière,* I, 8 (30 march 1851), pp. 29-30; and ". . . Séance du 4 avril 1851 . . . ," *La Lumière,* I, 10 (13 april 1851), pp. 37-38.

[4] Henry Sirodot, "Escalier de l'aile de François Ier au chateau de Blois. Vue photographique," *Revue générale de l'architecture et des travaux publics,* XIV (1856), col. 215.

[5] *Ibid.,* col. 215-216.

[6] Cited in Robin Middleton and David Watkin, *Neoclassical and 19th Century Architecture,* New York, 1980, pp. 370-371.

[7] I am indebted to Ms. Jean France for this observation.

[8] Henry Sirodot, "Les Halles Centrales à Paris. Vue du pavillon sud-ouest pendant le montage," *Revue générale de l'architecture et des travaux publics,* XIV (1856), col. 370, n. 1.

[9] *Ibid.,* col. 370.

[10] Charles Garnier, *A Travers les arts. Causeries et mélanges,* Paris, 1869, reprinted Paris, 1985, pp. 93-94.

[11] Louis Figuier, *La Photographie au Salon de 1859,* Paris, 1860, pp. 35-36.

[12] Théophile Gautier, in *La Presse,* 1850, cited in Sigfried Giedion, *Space, Time and Architecture: the Growth of a New Tradition,* Cambridge, 1956, p. 213.

[13] Victor Hugo, *Notre-Dame of Paris,* trans. by John Sturrock, New York, 1978, pp. 187-188.

I. ANTIQUITY AND ARCHAEOLOGY

*"It was said by Sir C. Wren, that 'the pursuit of Architecture was the study of antiquity rather than of fancy, and following that course must lead you back to the past.' . . . All men of reading desire to possess faithful representations of the monuments of antiquity—the pyramids of Gizeh, the palace of Carnac, or the Cyclopean walls of Greece. We feel a pure and healthful pleasure in examining even the images of scenes made sacred to our memory by the deeds of heroes or the words of sages. The temples of Athens, the wonderful Acropolis, the mysterious ruins of Paestum, and the fanes and arches of Rome, misnamed the Eternal, speak even from their pictures. . . . Each and all of these we are now able to preserve with the strictest fidelity, and impressed by the subtle finger of metal and glass, or on sheets of paper, every stone will tell its own tale, and as the mind of the poet shines for ever from his productions, so the very genius, the very spirit of the place, will speak to future ages as they now speak to us."—(*The Liverpool Photographic Journal, *1858.)*

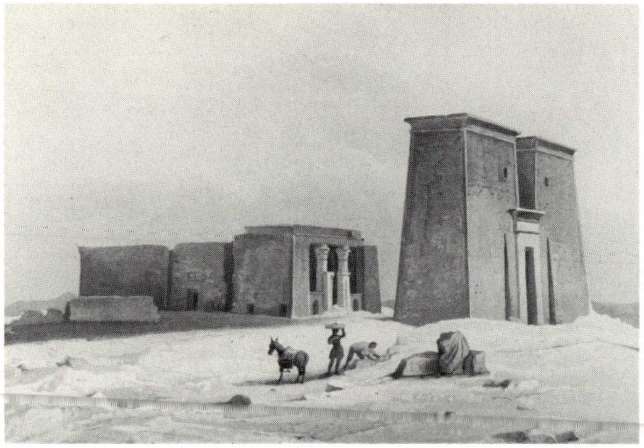

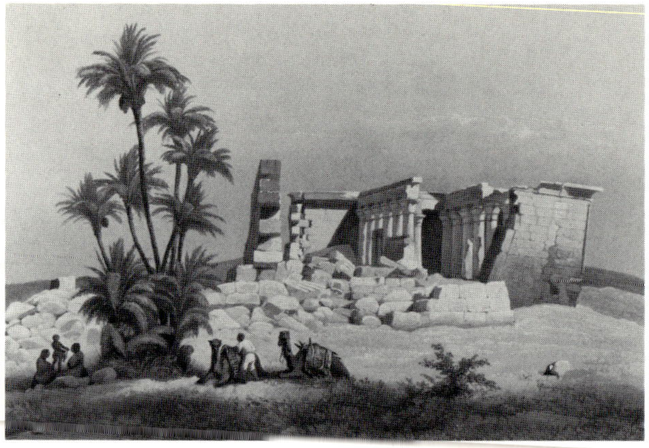

1. (PIERRE GUSTAVE JOLY DE LOTBINIERE)
Dakké and *Korti*

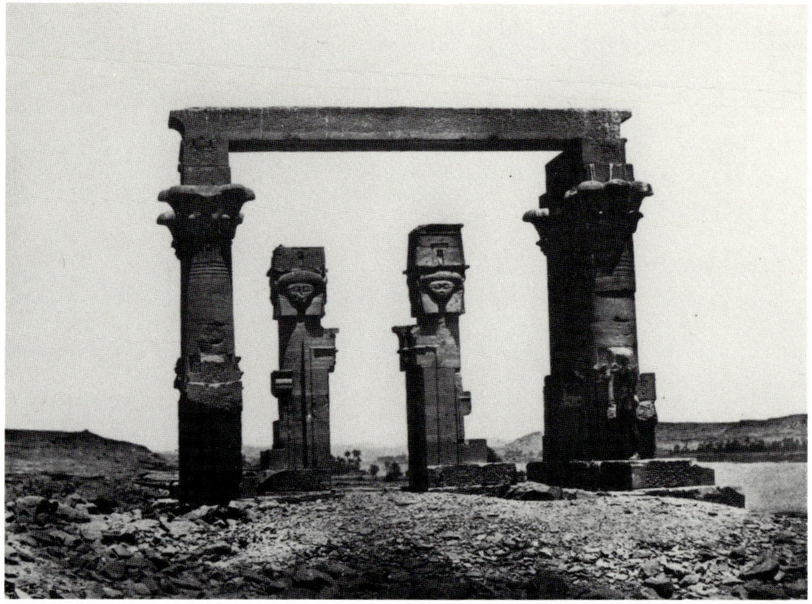

2. MAXIME DU CAMP
Nubia: Temple of Kardassy

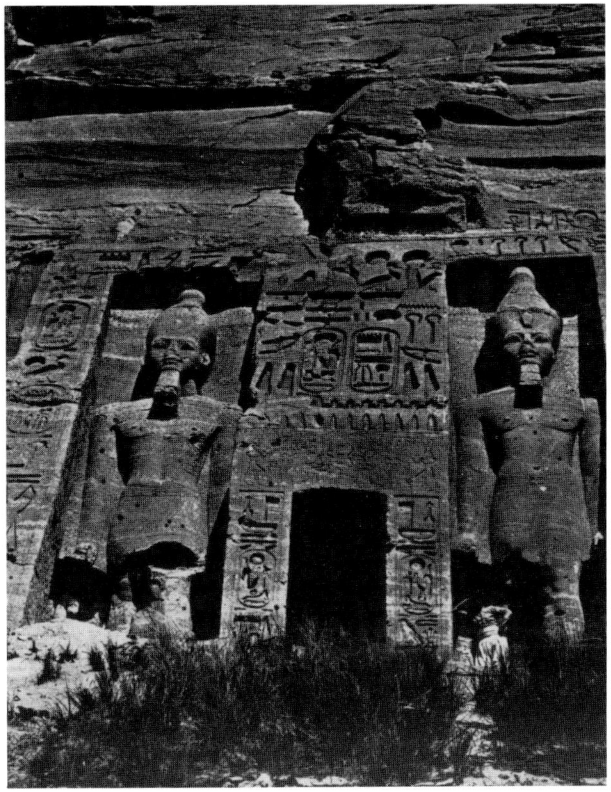

3. MAXIME DU CAMP
Nubia: Abu Simbel: Entrance of the Temple of Hathor

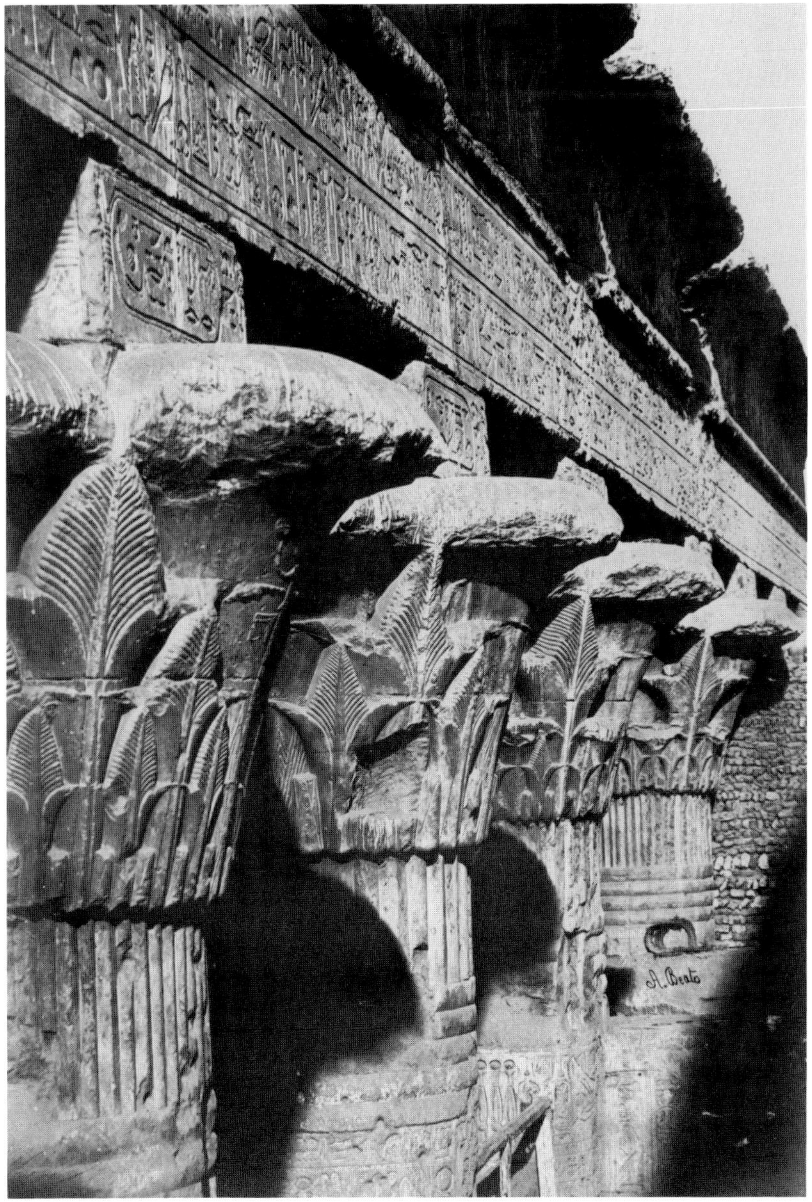

4. ANTONIO BEATO
Esne, Egypt: Temple of Khnum, Capitals of the Portico

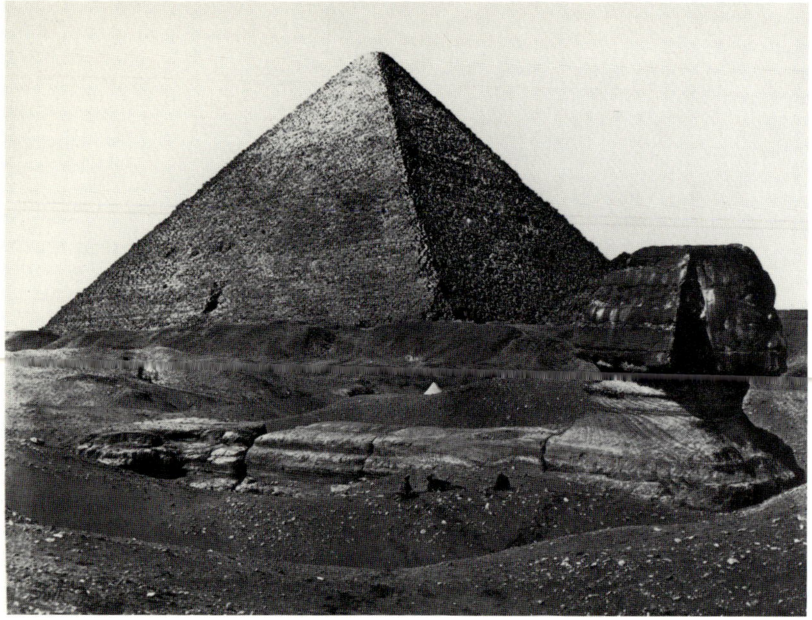

5. FRANCIS FRITH
The Great Pyramid, and the Great Sphinx

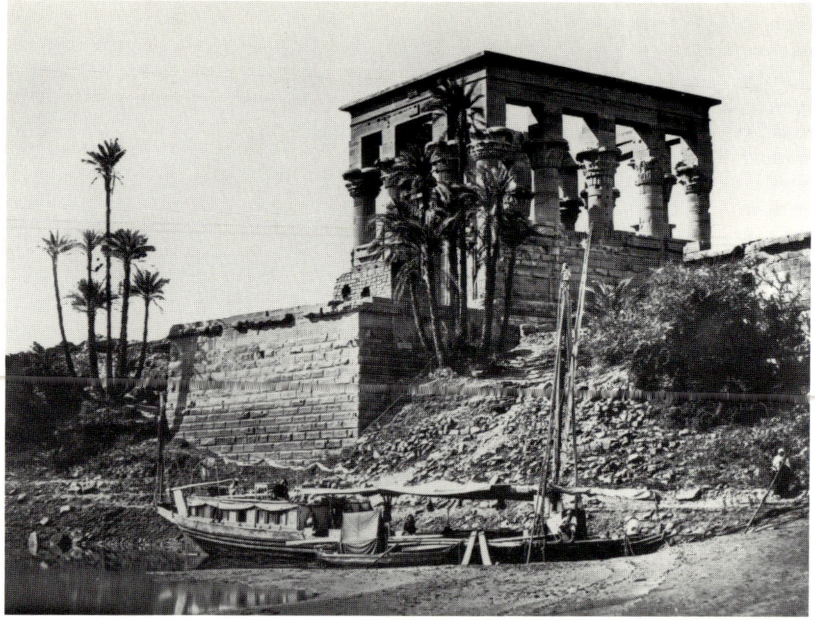

6. FRANCIS FRITH
The Hypaethral Temple, Philae

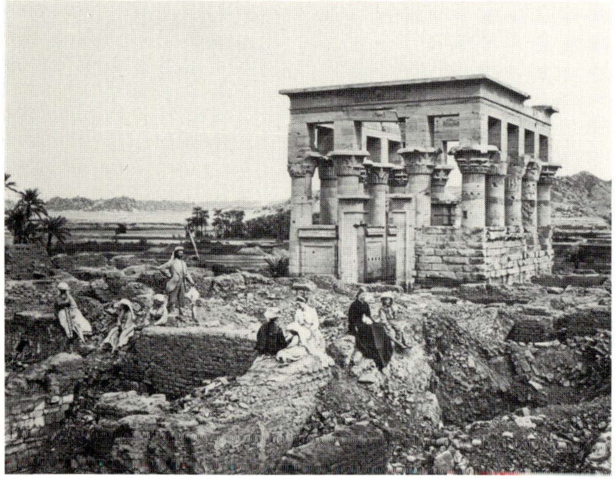

7. FRANK M. GOOD
Philae, Near View Hypaethral Temple

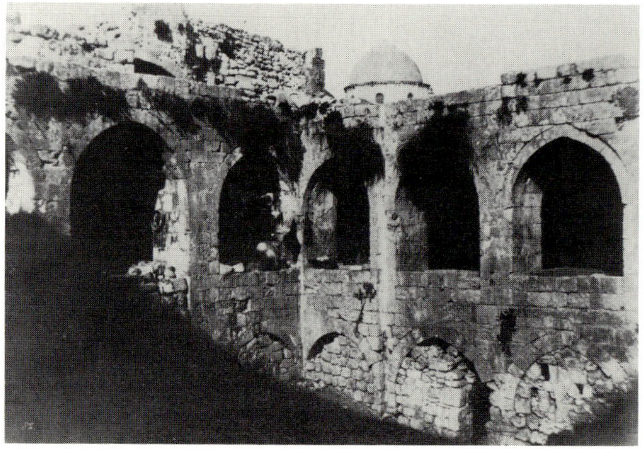

8. AUGUST SALZMANN
Temple Courtyard, Jerusalem

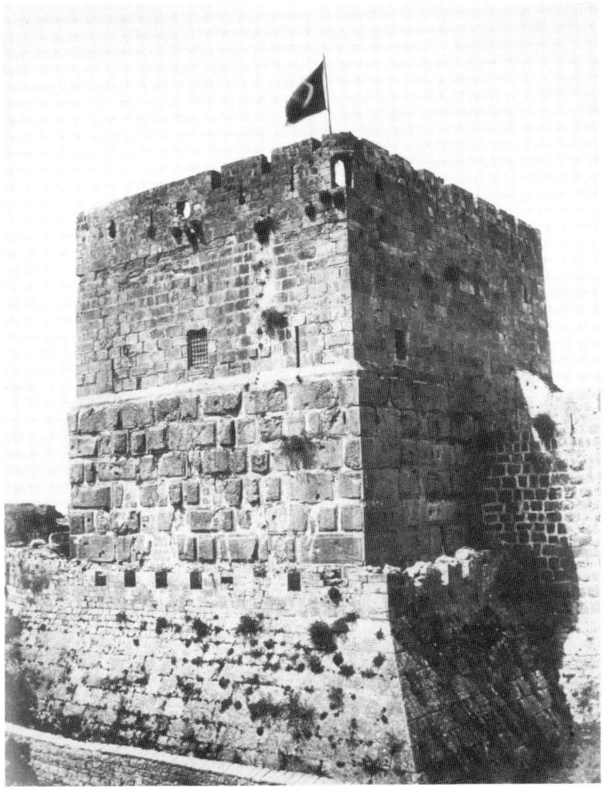

9. JAMES ROBERTSON and FELICE BEATO
The Tower of David, Jerusalem

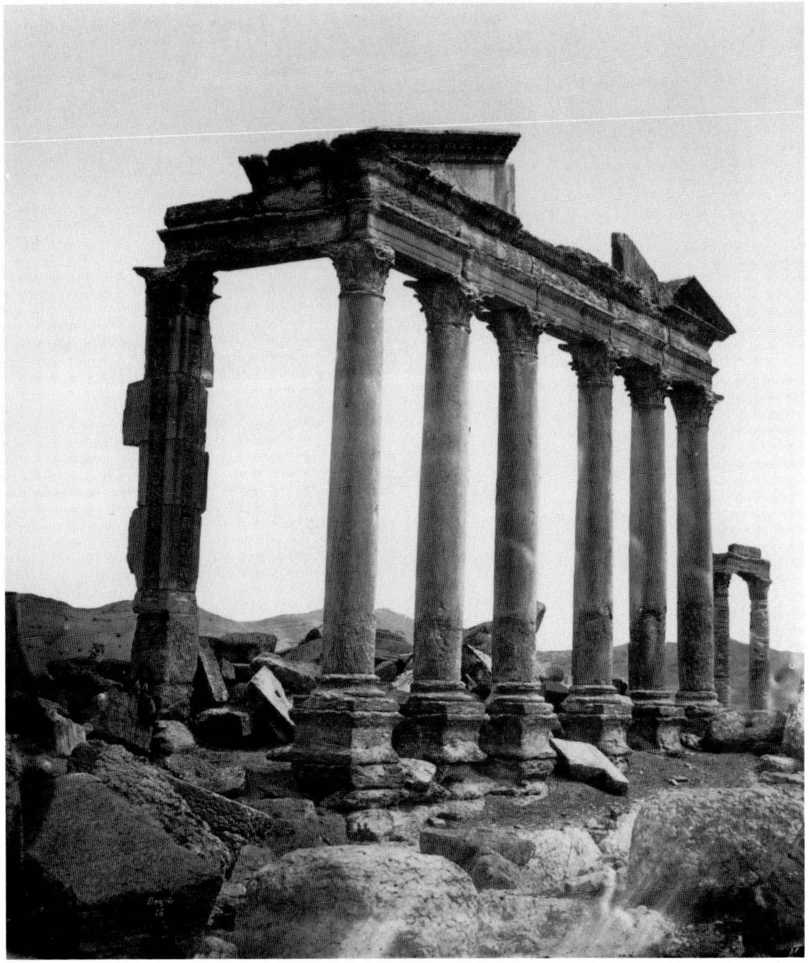

10. FELIX BONFILS
Palmyra: Ruins of the Southern End of a Temple (Syria)

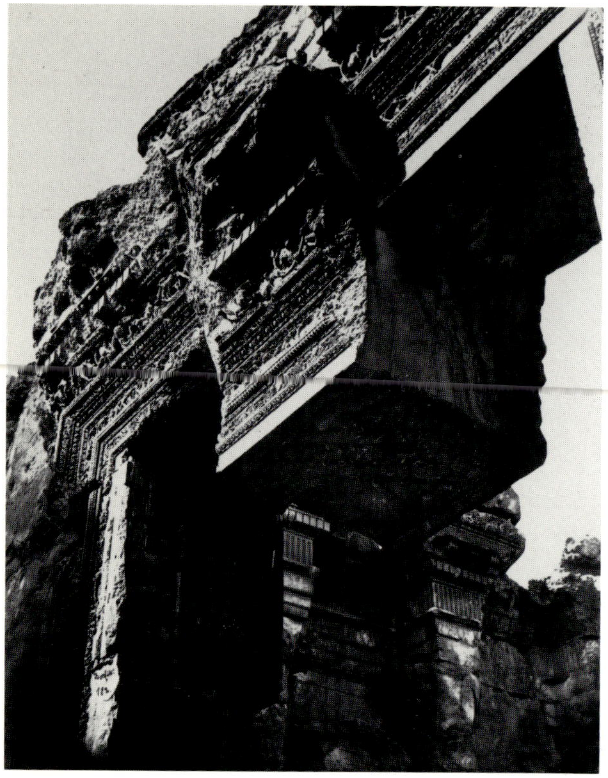

11. FELIX BONFILS
Baalbek: Portal of the Temple of Jupiter (Syria)

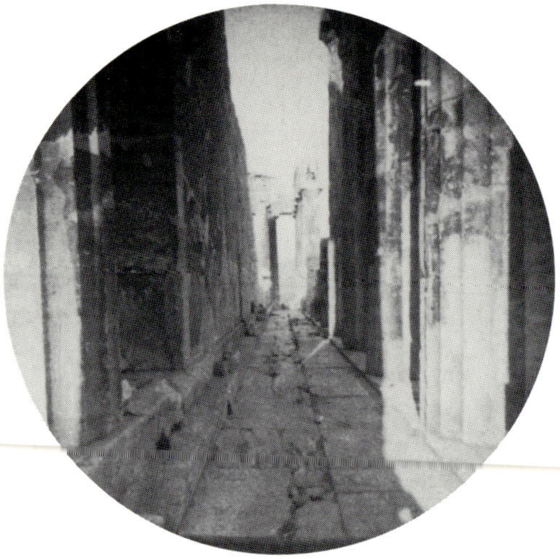

12. UNIDENTIFIED PHOTOGRAPHER
a. *Parthenon Colonnade, Athens*

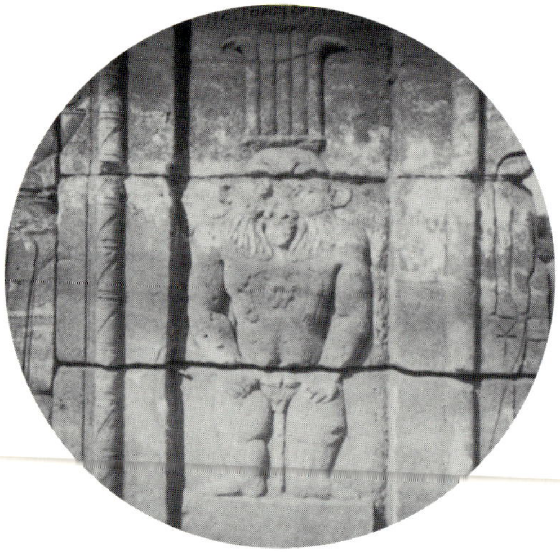

b. *Devil at Entrance, Temple Mute*

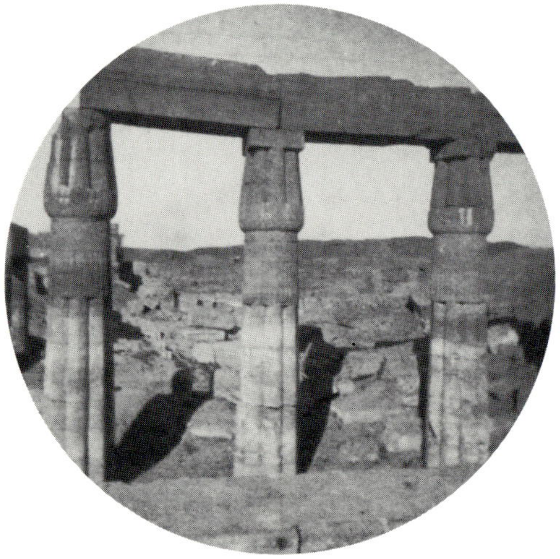

c. *Lotus Columns, Temple Thothmes III, Karnak*

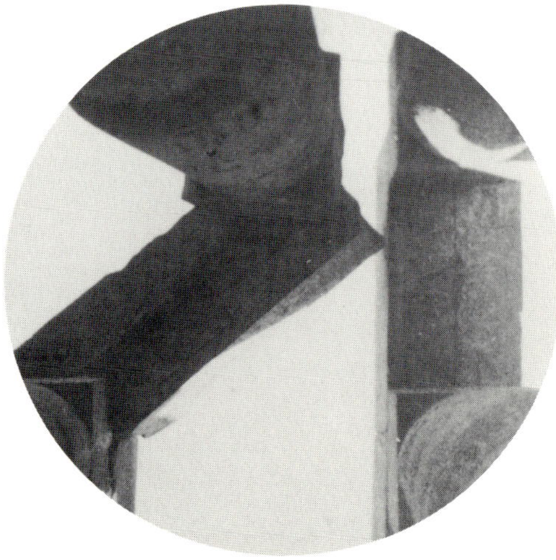

d. *Looking Up at Leaning Columns at Karnak*

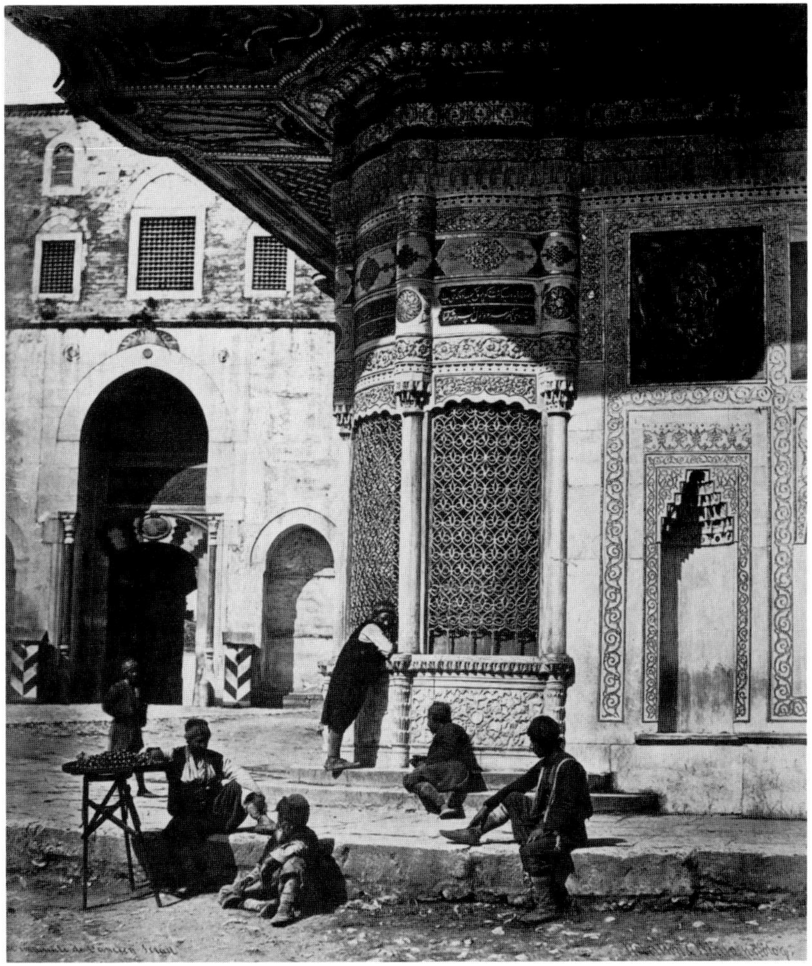

13. JAMES ROBERTSON and FELICE BEATO
Imperial Door of the Old Seraglio—Constantinople

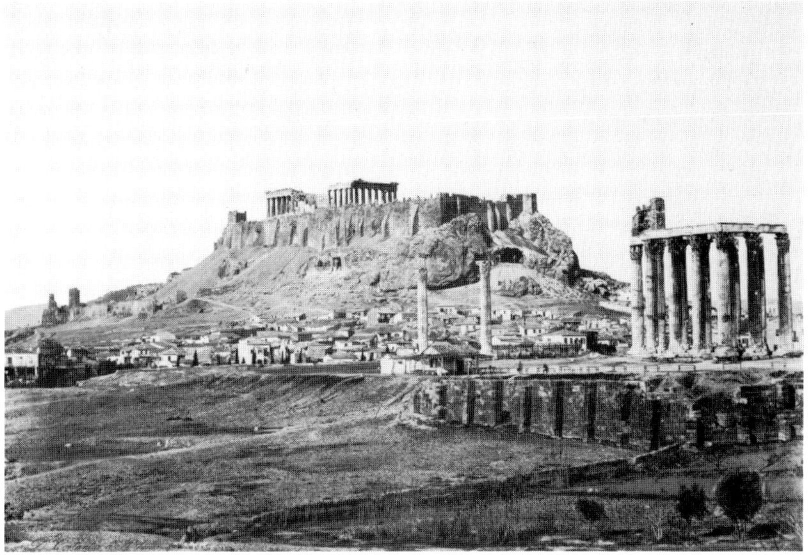

14. D. CONSTANTINE (or COSTANTIN)
The Acropolis at Athens, with the Temple of Jupiter

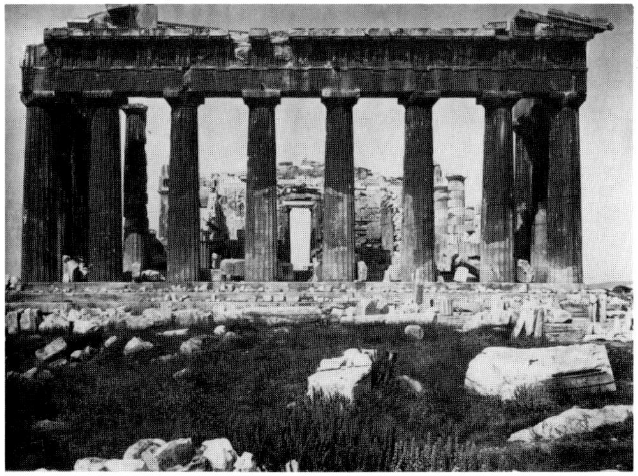

15. WILLIAM JAMES STILLMAN
View of the Parthenon, Athens

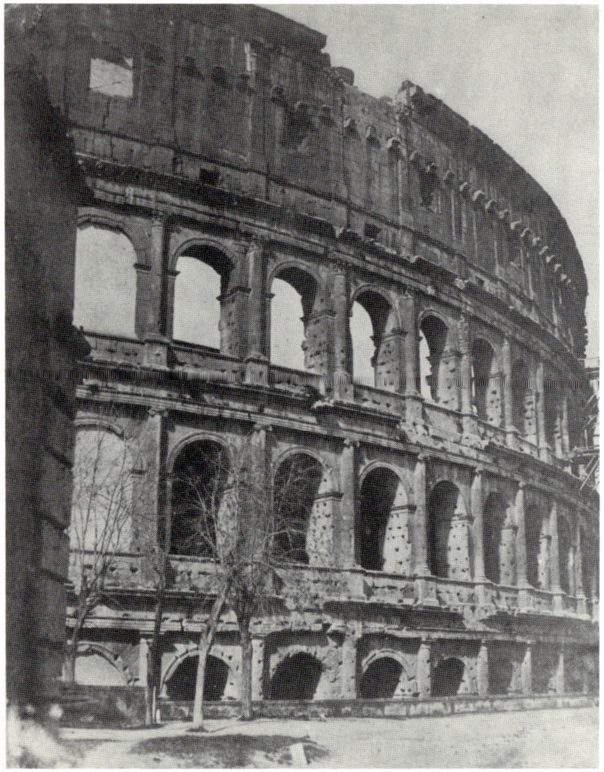

16. (REVEREND CALVERT R. JONES)
The Colosseum

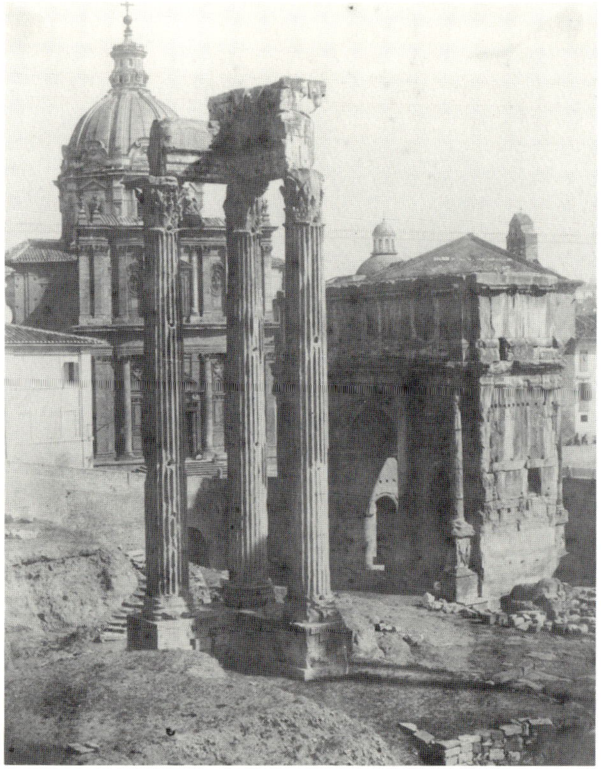

17. COUNT FREDERIC A. FLACHERON
The Roman Forum

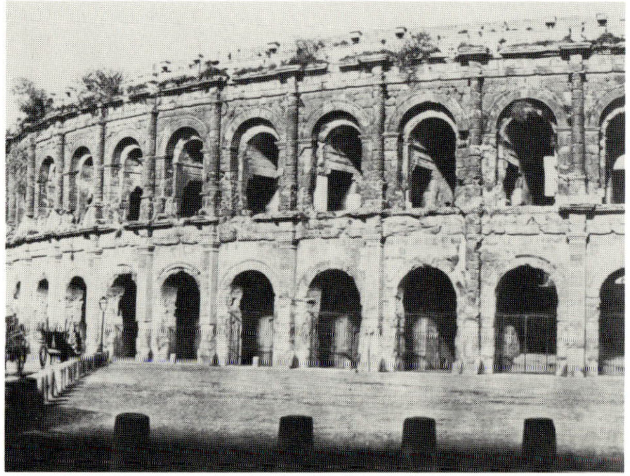

18. EDOUARD-DENIS BALDUS
Amphitheater at Nimes

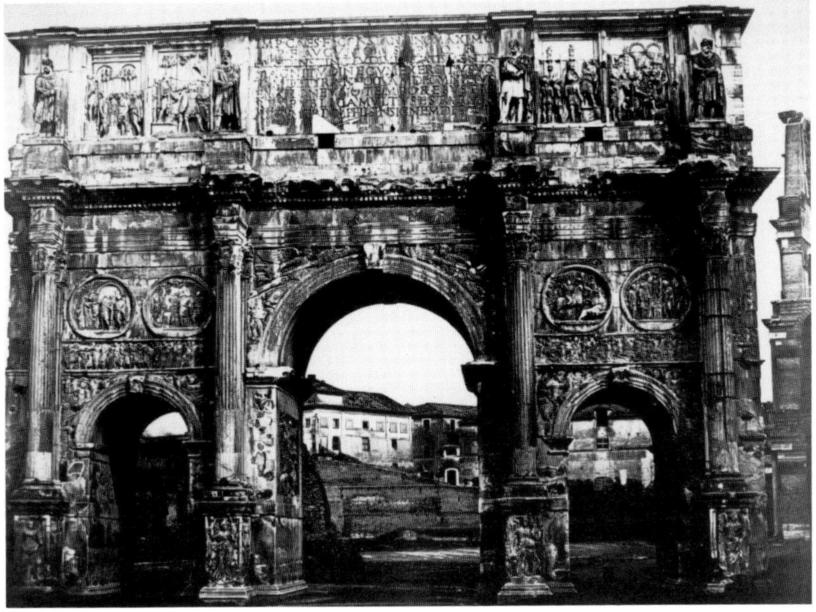

19. ROBERT MACPHERSON
Arch of Constantine—South Facade

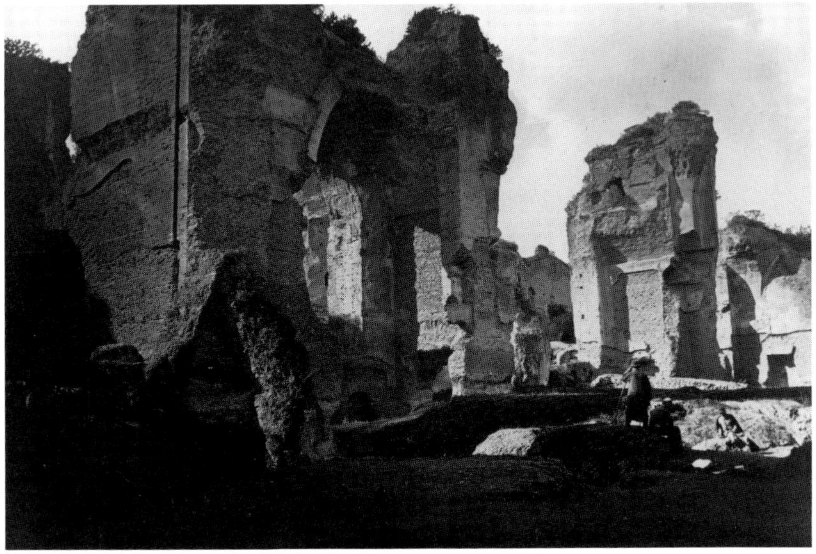

21. GIOACCHINO ALTOBELLI (and POMPEO MOLINS ?)
Ruins of the Thermae of Caracalla

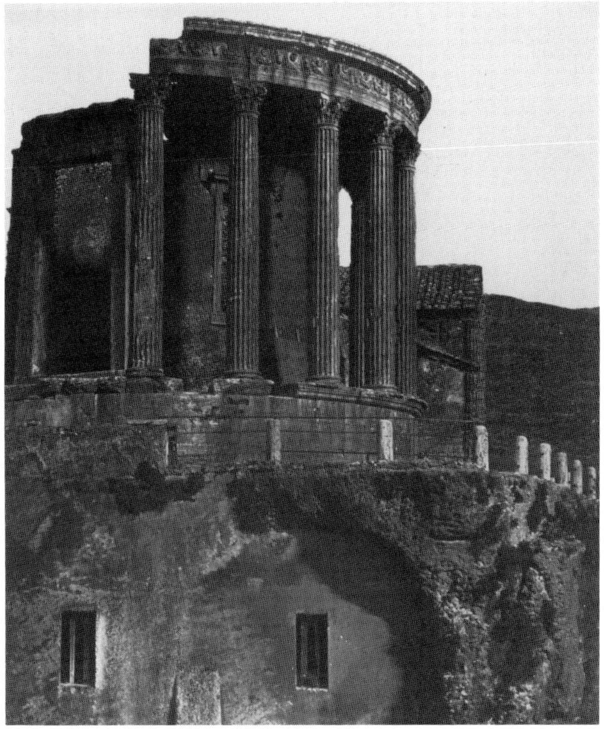

20. ROBERT MACPHERSON
Temple of the Sibyl at Tivoli

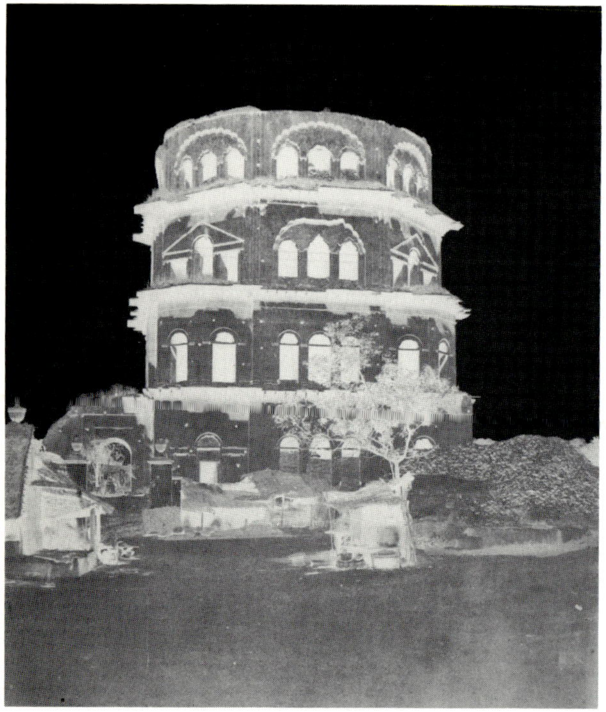

22a. UNIDENTIFIED PHOTOGRAPHER
Inside View of the Principal Entrance of the Jumma Musjid

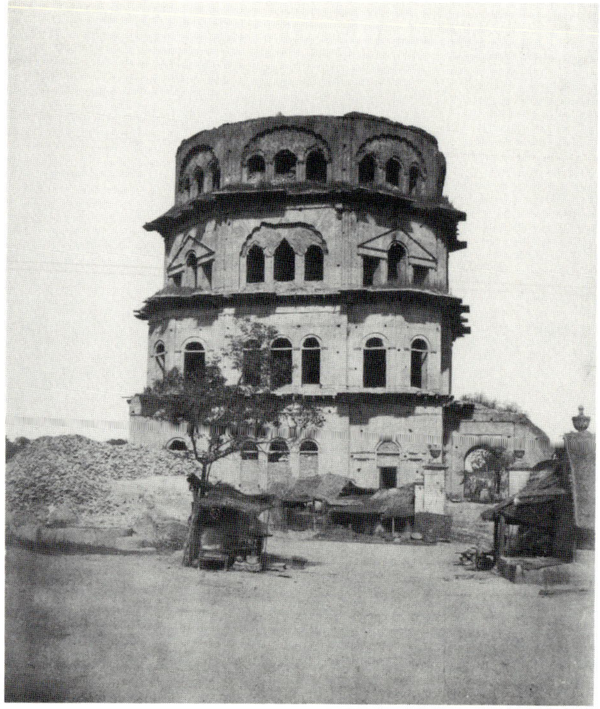

22b. UNIDENTIFIED PHOTOGRAPHER
Inside View of the Principal Entrance of the Jumma Musjid

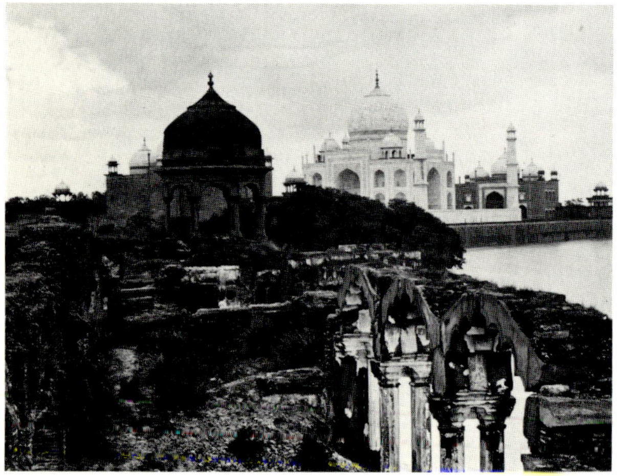

23. LIEUTENANT SENIOR
The Taj Mahal, Agra

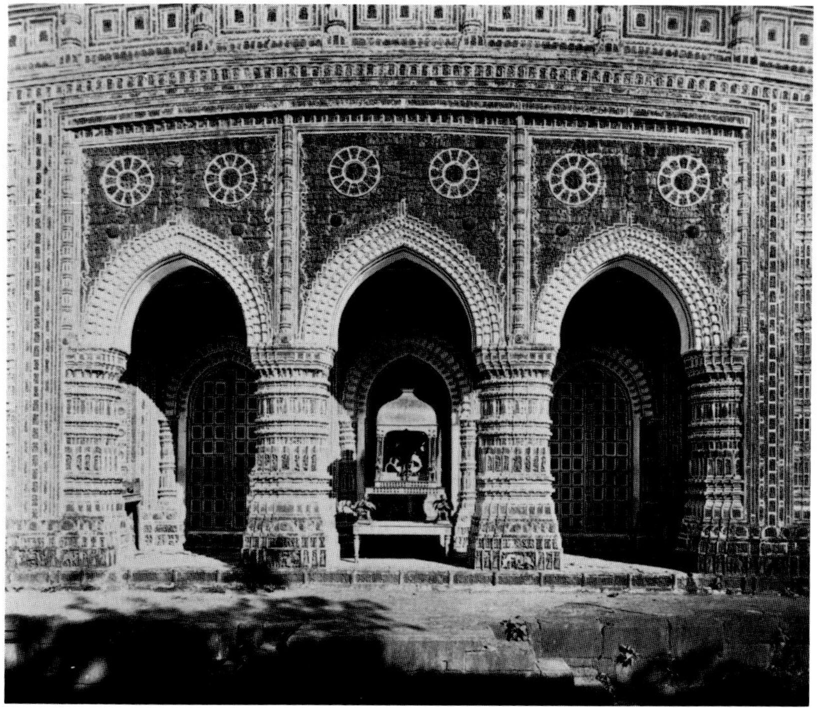

24. UNIDENTIFIED PHOTOGRAPHER
Entry Portal, India

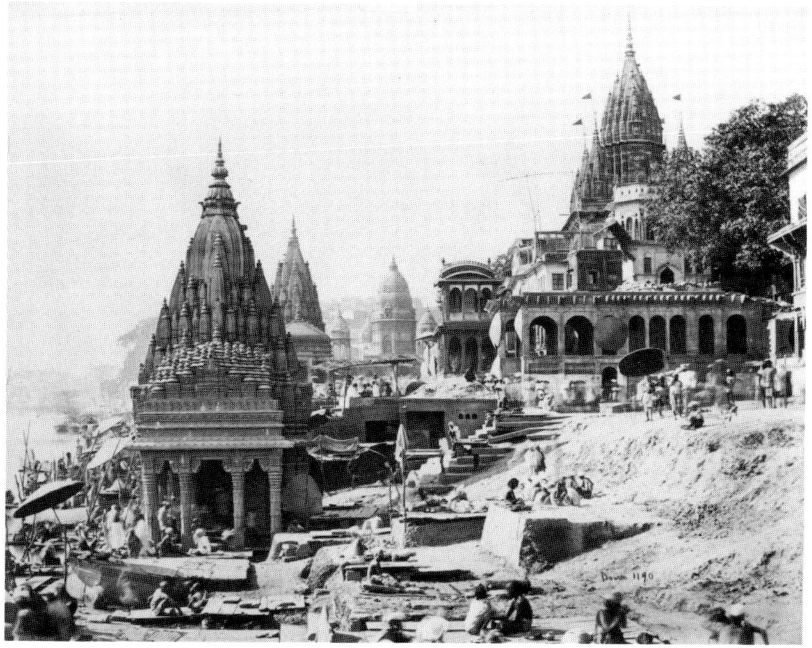

25. SAMUEL BOURNE
Benares: Vishnu Pud and Other Temples Near the Burning Ghât

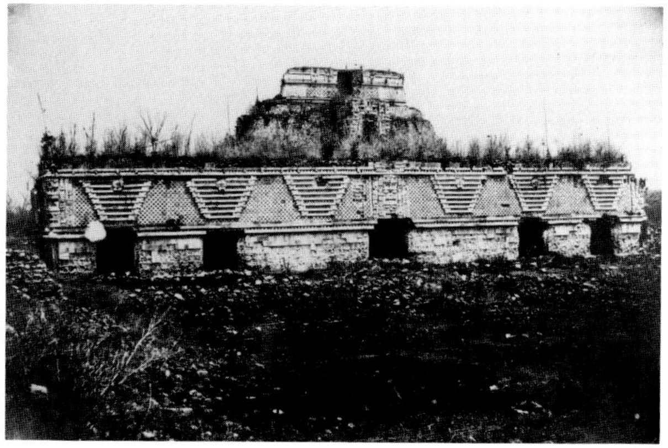

26. CLAUDE-JOSEPH-DESIRE CHARNAY
Nunnery, Uxmal, Mexico

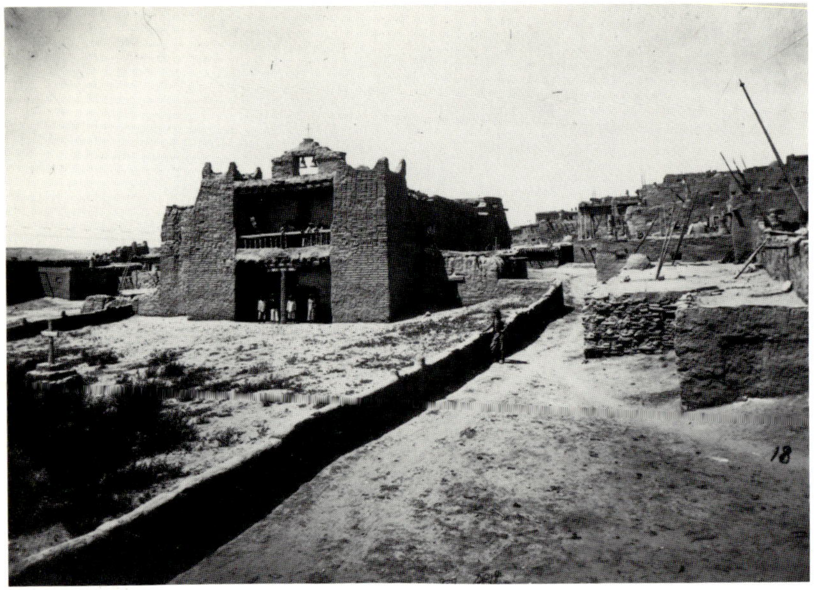

27. TIMOTHY O'SULLIVAN
Old Mission Church, Zuni Pueblo, N.M., View from the Plaza

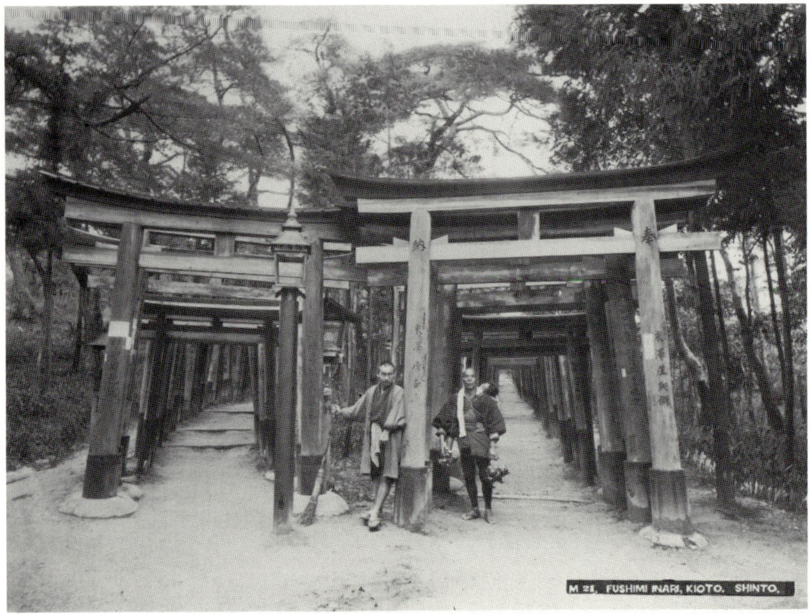

28. UNIDENTIFIED PHOTOGRAPHER
Fushimi Inari, Kioto, Shinto

II. EUROPEAN HISTORY

"One of the most precious practical results stemming from photography's invention has been the swift popular appreciation of all the monuments of different countries. Practical processes of paper photography were scarcely developed, when a phalanx of operators scattered in all directions, cameras in hand, to bring us views of monuments, edifices, and ruins from every land of the known world. The result: a series of collections that, under the title Photographic Voyages, *offered us authentic specimens of ancient and modern monuments dispersed across the globe. Thus, without leaving one's residence or even one's fireplace, one could enjoy the spectacles or devote oneself to studies that until then had been the exclusive privilege of a few happy travelers—it is the world in a portfolio or, to use Alfred de Musset's expression, the spectacle in an armchair."*

—*(Louis Figuier [critic], 1859)*

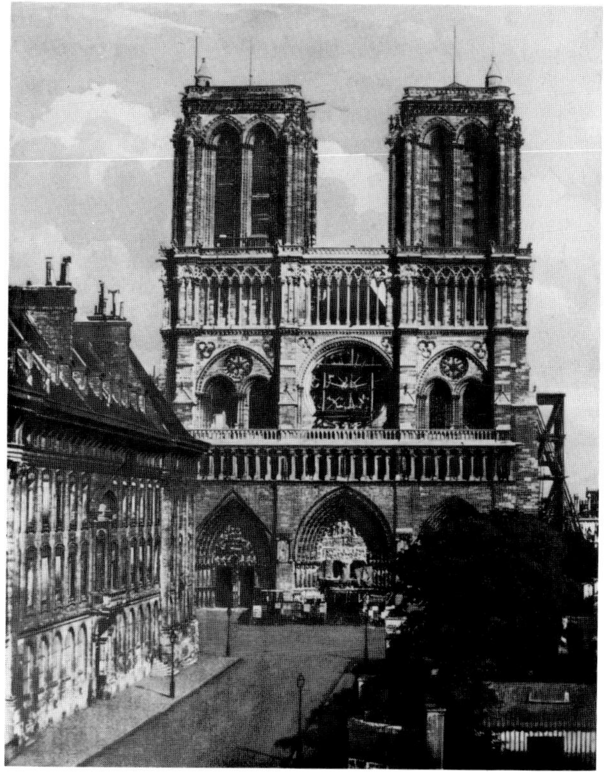

29. LOUIS-AUGUSTE and AUGUSTE-ROSALIE BISSON
Notre-Dame of Paris

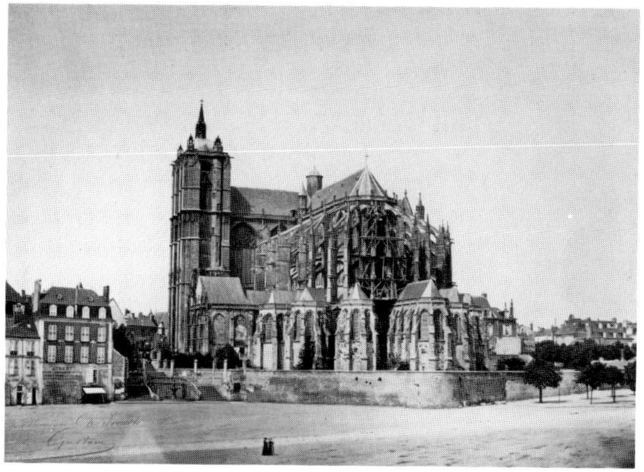

30. GUSTAVE (?)
Cathedral of Saint Julien, Le Mans, from Place des Jacobins

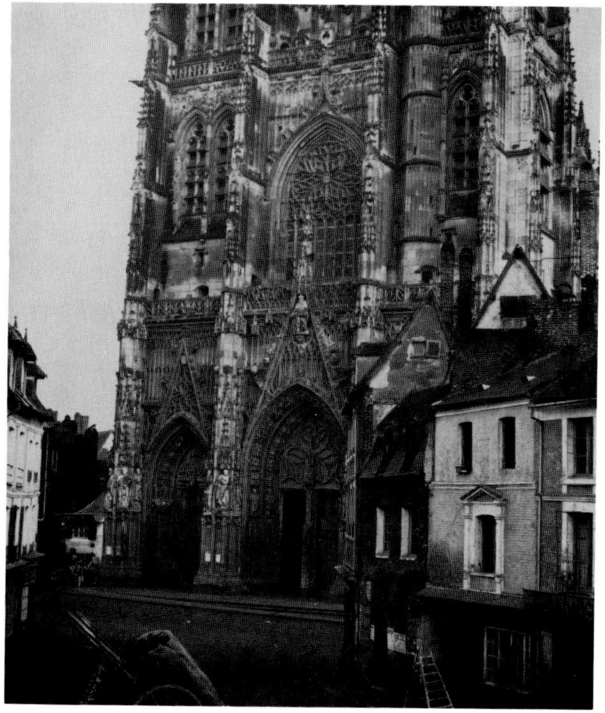

31. LOUIS-AUGUSTE and AUGUSTE-ROSALIE BISSON
Saint Vulfran, Abbeville, Western Façade

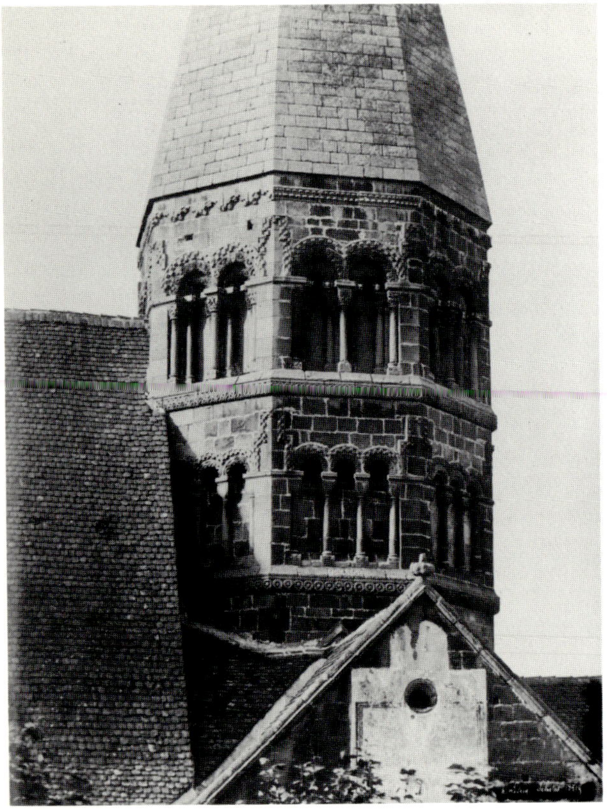

32. HENRI DESTOURNELLES LE SECQ
Selestat: Eglise St. Georges

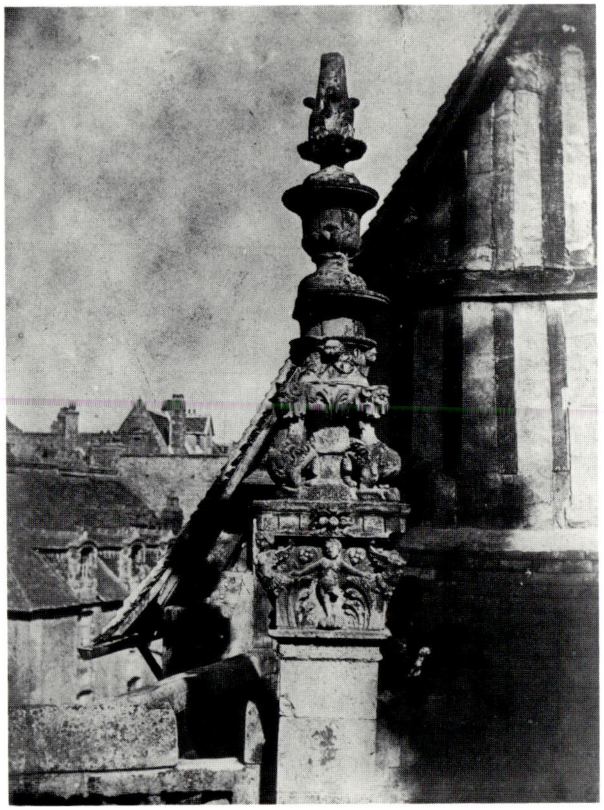

34. (LOUIS-DESIRE BLANQUART-EVRARD)
Turret Finial, St. Pierre, Caen

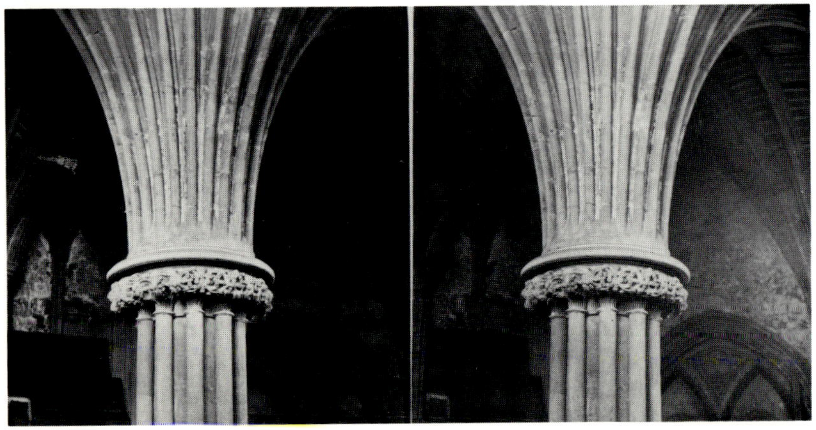

33. ALEXANDER WILSON
Lichfield Cathedral: The Center Pillar in the Chapter House

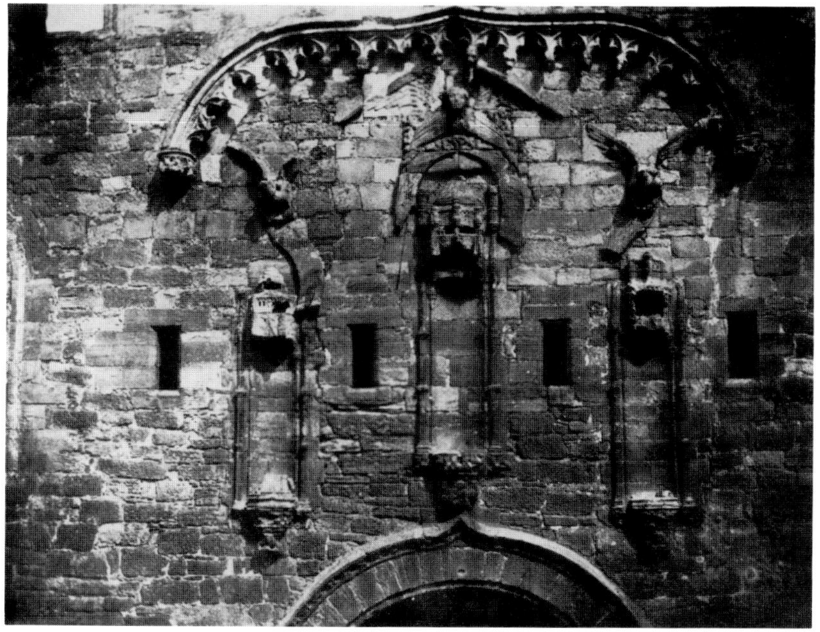

35. DAVID OCTAVIUS HILL (and) ROBERT ADAMSON
Linlithgow Palace, Niches Over the Entrance

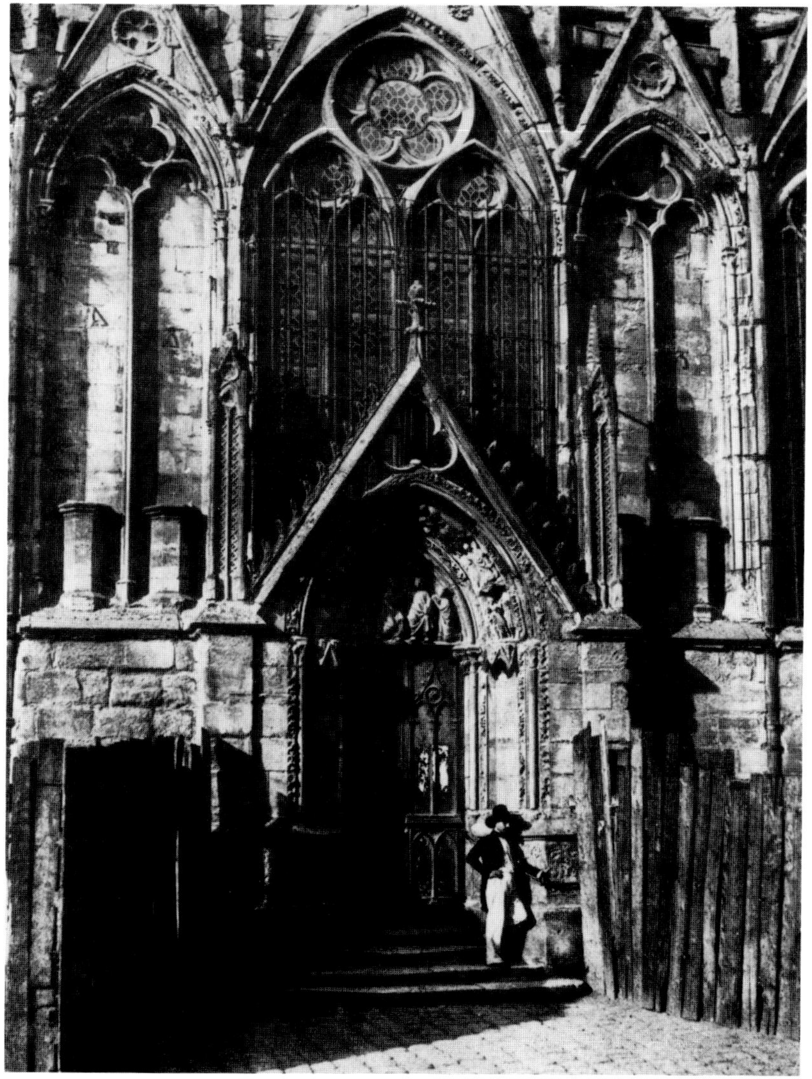

36. CHARLES MARVILLE
The Red Door. Northern Doorway of Notre-Dame, Paris

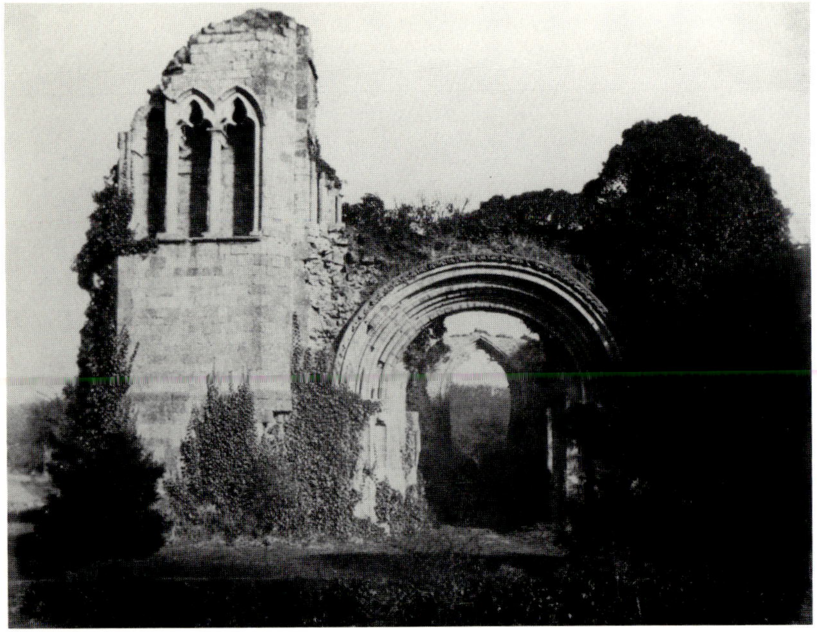

37. CHARLES CHENEY
Tilleshall Abbey

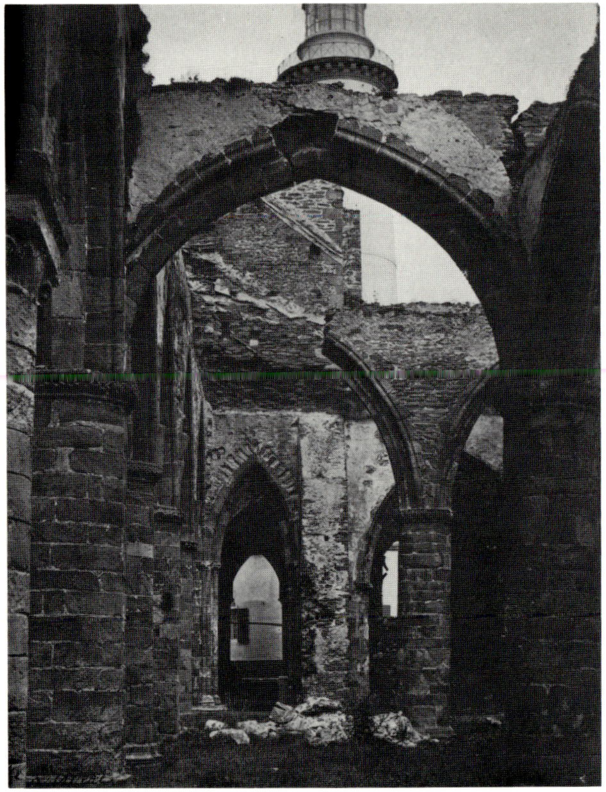

38. GENEVIEVE-ELISABETH DISDERI
Interior of St. Mathieu

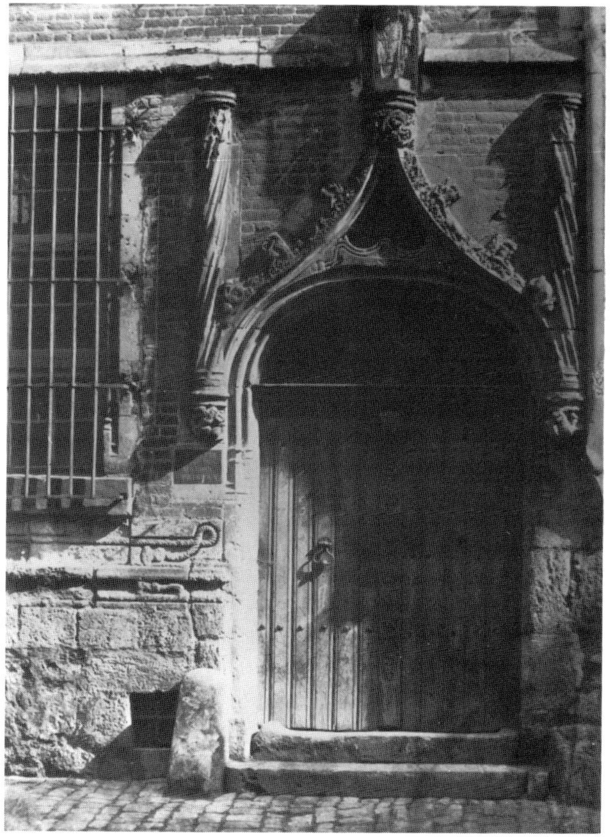

39. GABRIEL BLAASE
Portal of the Maison Tristan

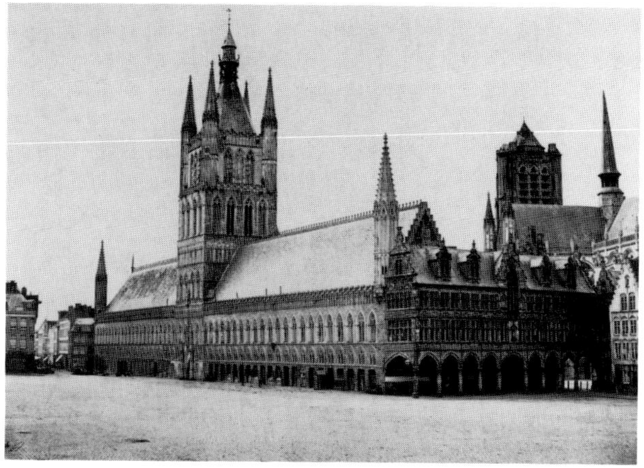

40. LOUIS-AUGUSTE and AUGUSTE-ROSALIE BISSON
Guildhall, Yprès

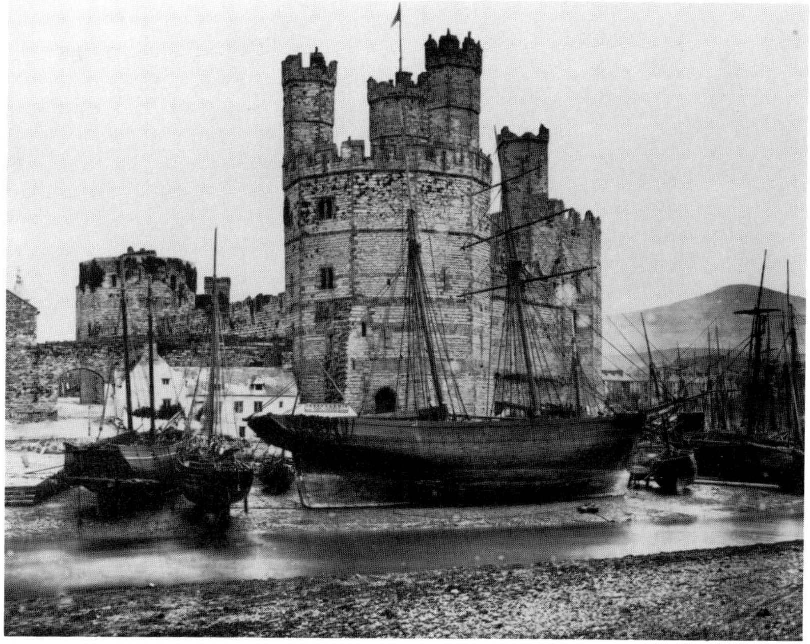

41. R. MURRAY
Carnarvon Castle

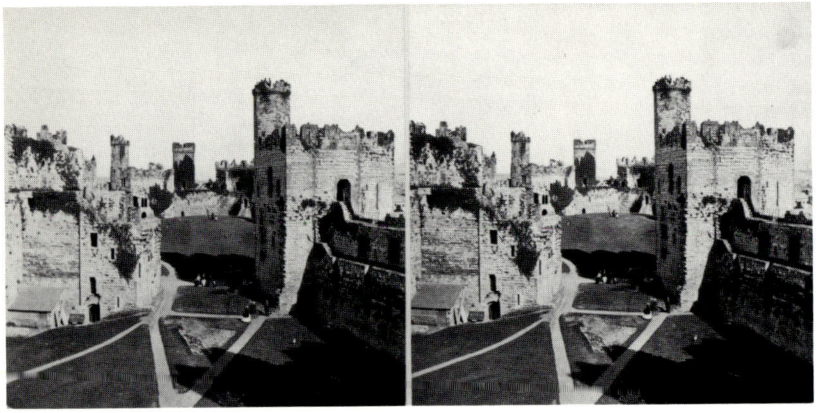

42. FRANCIS BEDFORD
Carnarvon Castle, Interior, from the Eagle Tower

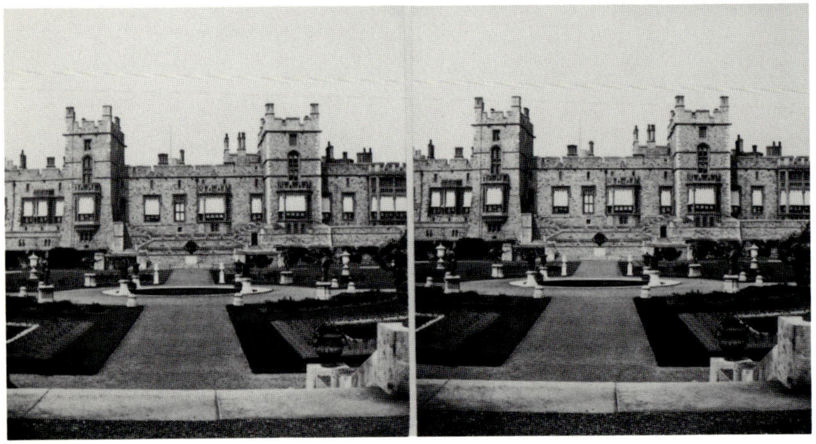

43. GEORGE WASHINGTON WILSON
Windsor Castle, The Garden Terrace

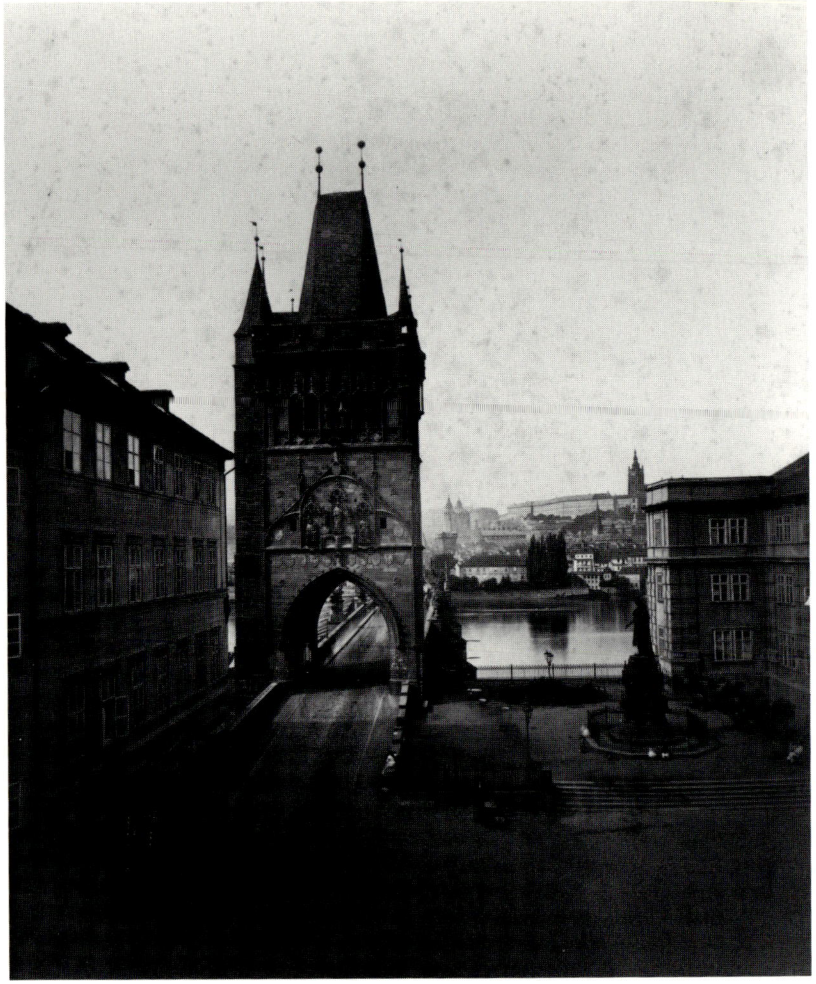

44. FRANTISEK JOSEF FRIDRICH
Prague: Tower Bridge, Old City

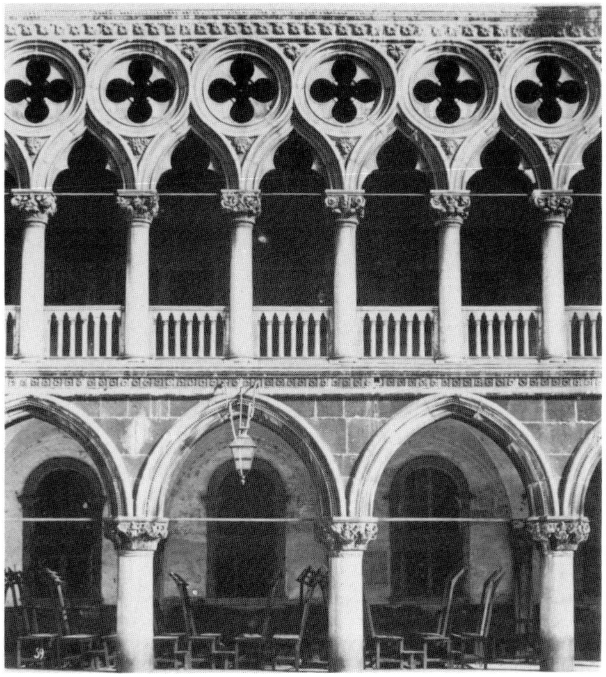

45. (CARLO PONTI)
Detail of the Ducal Palace, Venice

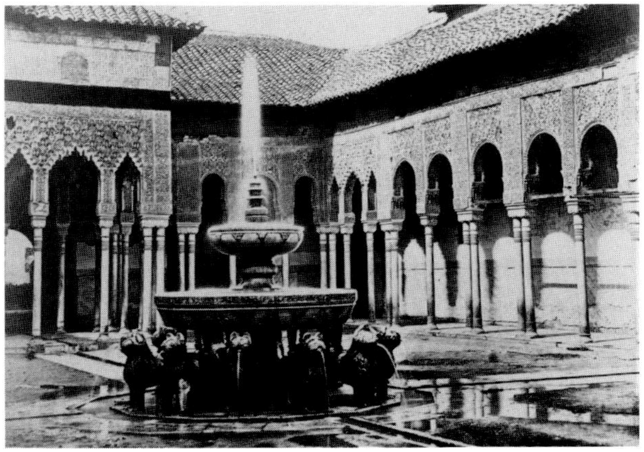

46. CHARLES CLIFFORD
Patio of the Léones y Fuente, The Alhambra

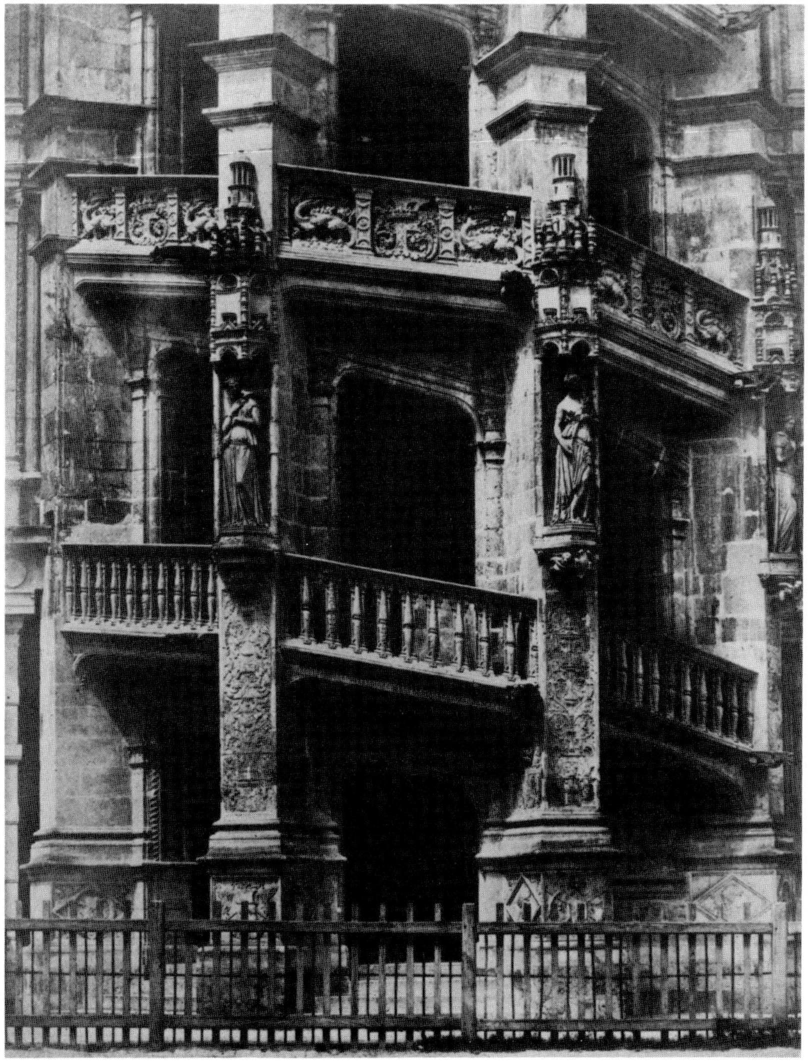

47. (FR. ALPH. FORTIER)
François I Wing and Staircase, Chateau de Blois

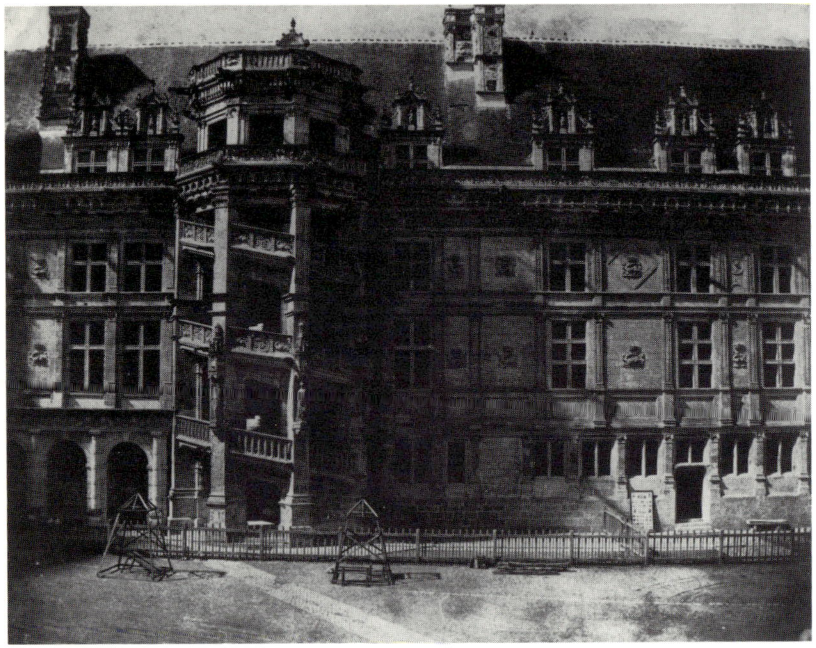

48. (LOUIS-DESIRE BLANQUART-EVRARD)
François I Wing and Staircase, Chateau de Blois

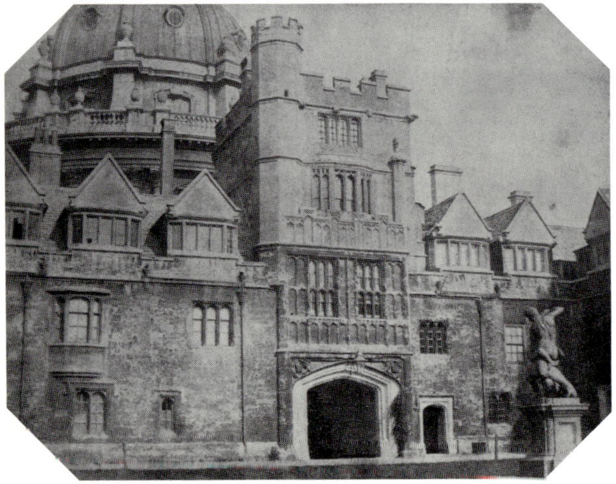

49. WILLIAM HENRY FOX TALBOT
Oxford

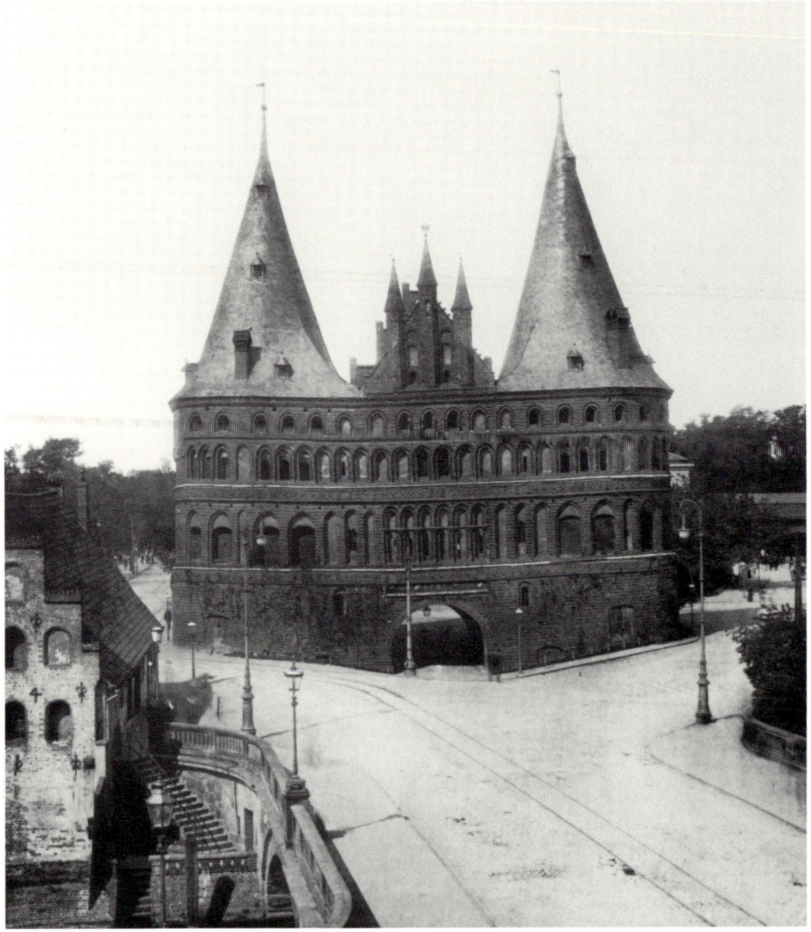

50. UNIDENTIFIED PHOTOGRAPHER
Holstentor, Lübeck

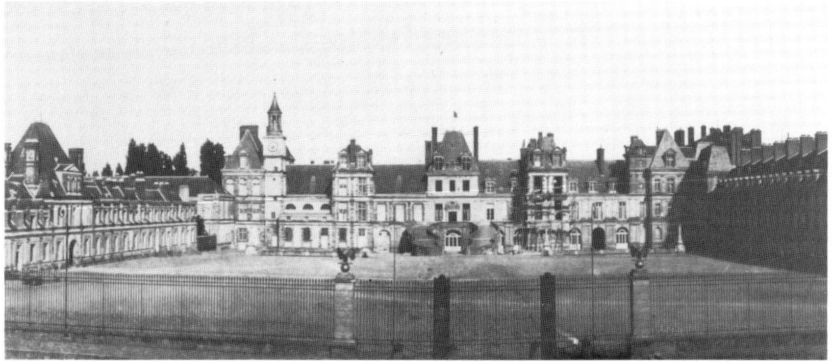

51. LADISLAS CHODZKIEWICZ
Courtyard of Farewells, Palais de Fontainebleau

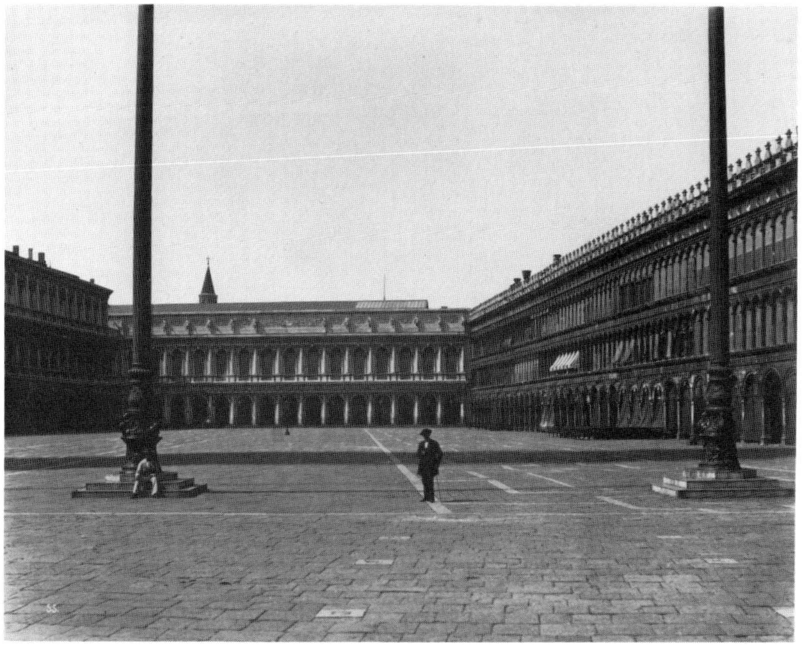

52. (CARLO PONTI)
View of the Piazza di San Marco

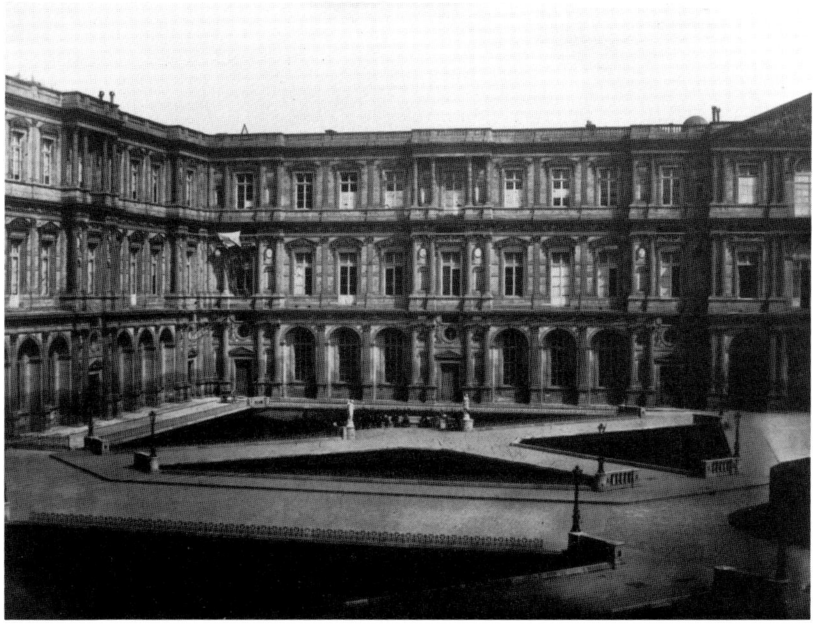

53. (FR. ALPH. FORTIER)
Interior of the Louvre Courtyard

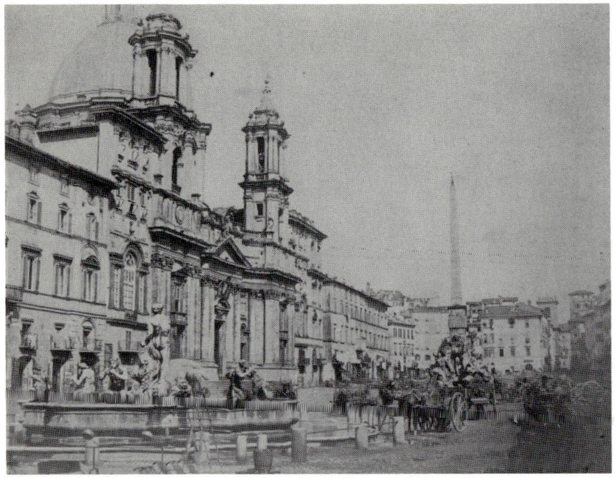

54. (REVEREND CALVERT R. JONES)
View of the Piazza Navona, Rome

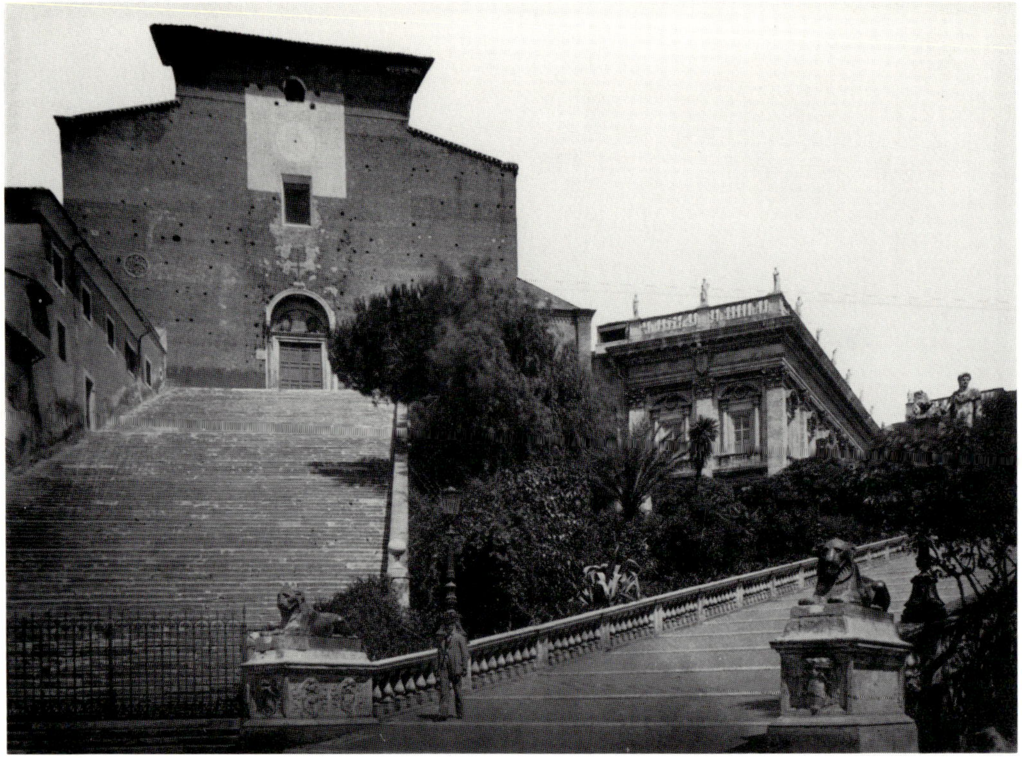

55. JAMES ANDERSON
Santa Maria in Aracoeli, Rome

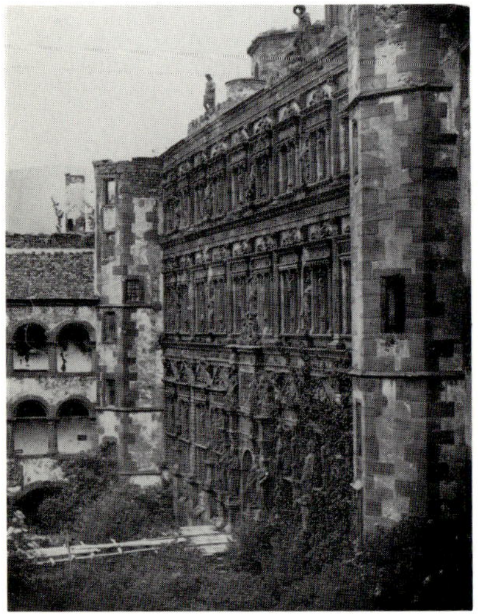

56. LOUIS-AUGUSTE and
AUGUSTE-ROSALIE BISSON
Tournament Court, Castle of Heidelberg

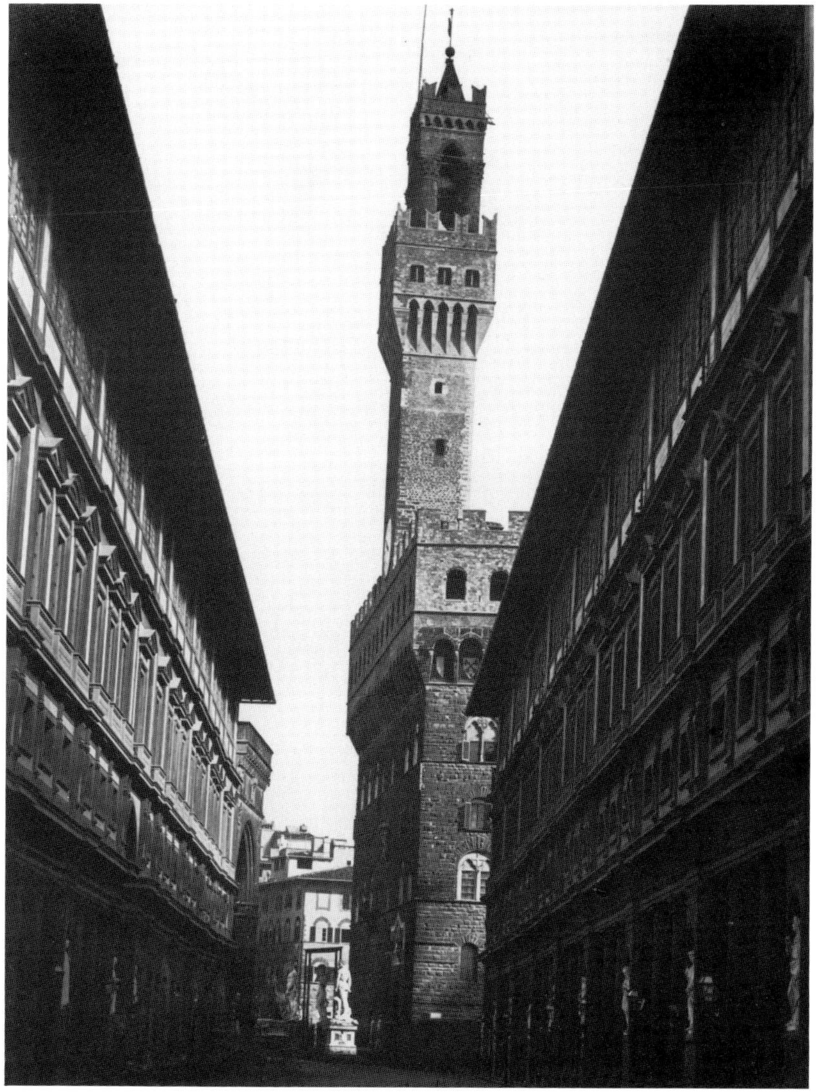

57. LEOPOLDO, ROMUALDO, and GIUSEPPE ALINARI
Florence: The Piazzale degli Uffizi

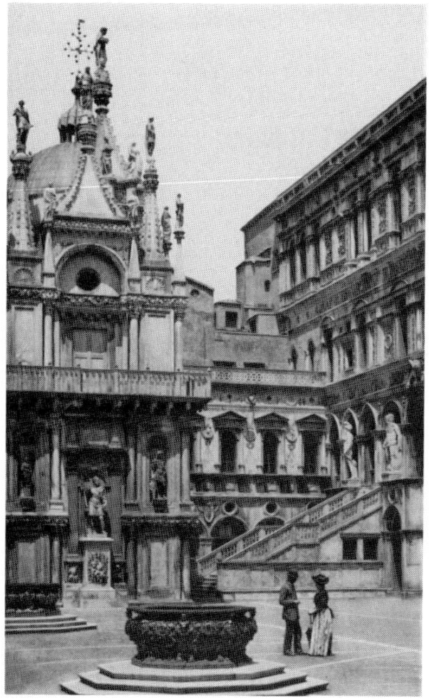

58. FERDINANDO ONGANIA
Courtyard of the Ducal Palace and the Giants' Staircase

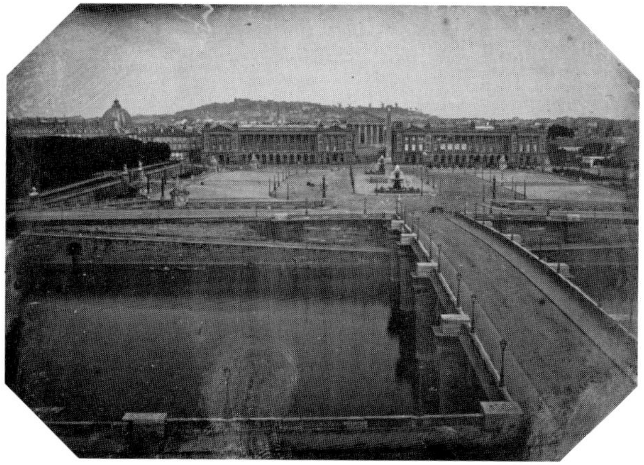

59. UNIDENTIFIED PHOTOGRAPHER
The Place de la Concorde, Paris

III. CONTEMPORARY ARCHITECTURAL EXPRESSIONS

"It is true that the photographer cannot compose; however, if he makes a portrait, he must pose his model in such a way as to set off his or her beauty, if there are any, or at least diminish his or her imperfections. He must also illuminate the model tastefully, in order to gain a good effect and to give the model an advantageous expression. If it is a question of reproducing a monument, other difficulties present themselves. Each monument has, as it were, its own lighting. . . . One church must be reproduced in full sunlight; another only under an overcast sky and with diffused lighting. The photographer must therefore choose his hour and, even more, his position in order to obtain the most beautiful ensemble and the most perfect lines. For this, it is absolutely necessary that he have the sentiment of the beautiful which is to say, he must be an artist."—(Ernest Lacan [critic], 1856)

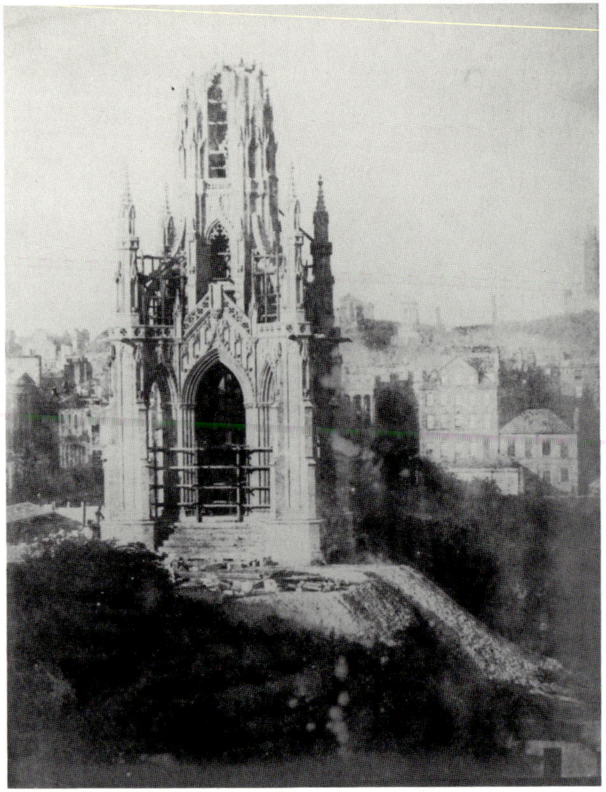

60. DAVID OCTAVIUS HILL and ROBERT ADAMSON
Sir Walter Scott Monument, Edinburgh, Under Construction

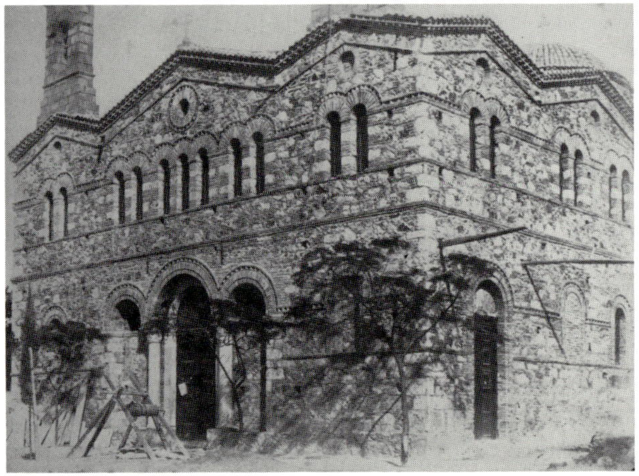

61. JOHN SHAW SMITH
Modern Church in Athens

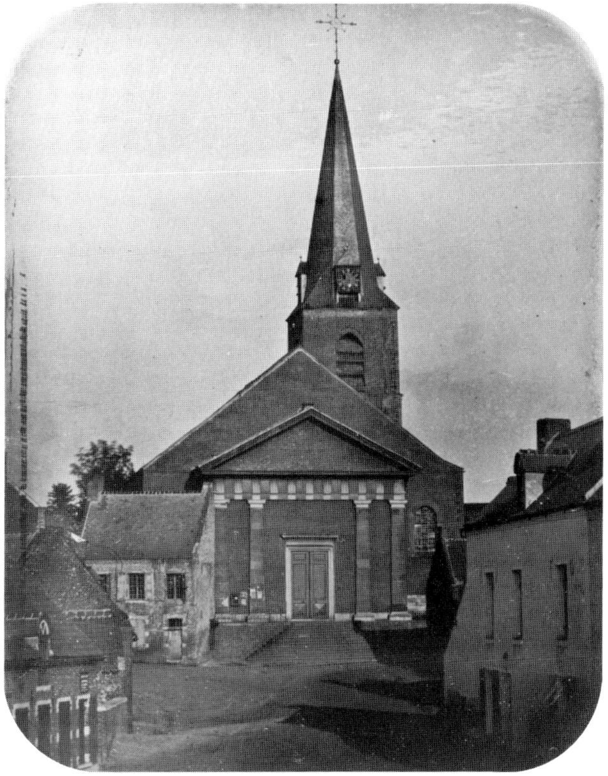

62. UNIDENTIFIED PHOTOGRAPHER
Church with "Doric" Façade

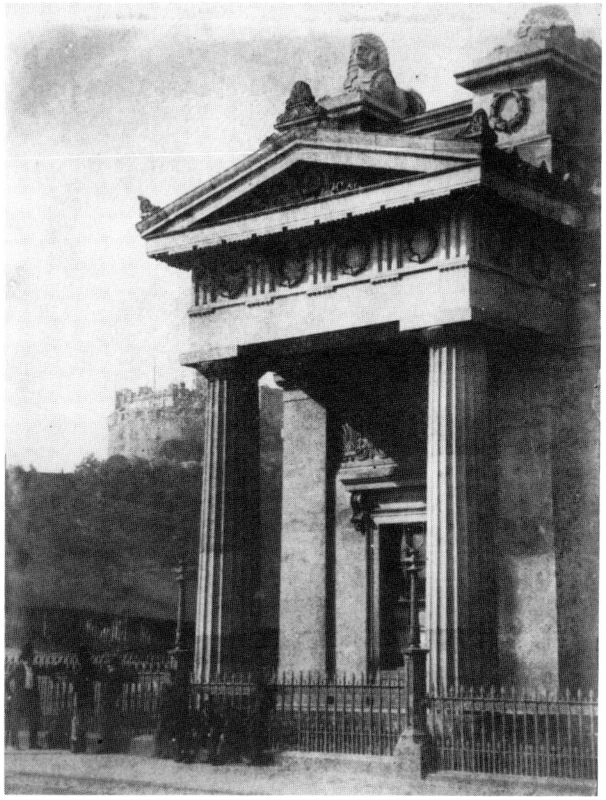

63. DAVID OCTAVIUS HILL and ROBERT ADAMSON
The Royal Institution with the Castle in the Background

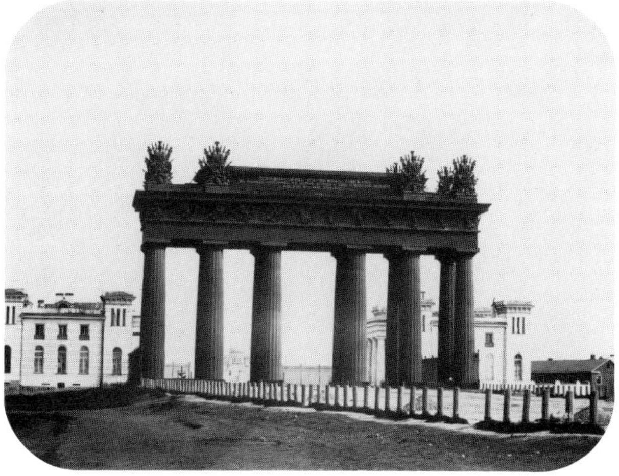

64. HUARD
Arch of Triumph, St. Petersburg, 1838

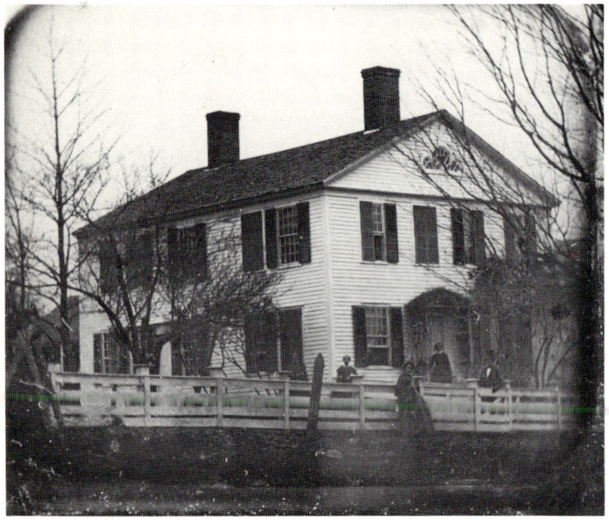

65. UNIDENTIFIED PHOTOGRAPHER
A Rural Residence

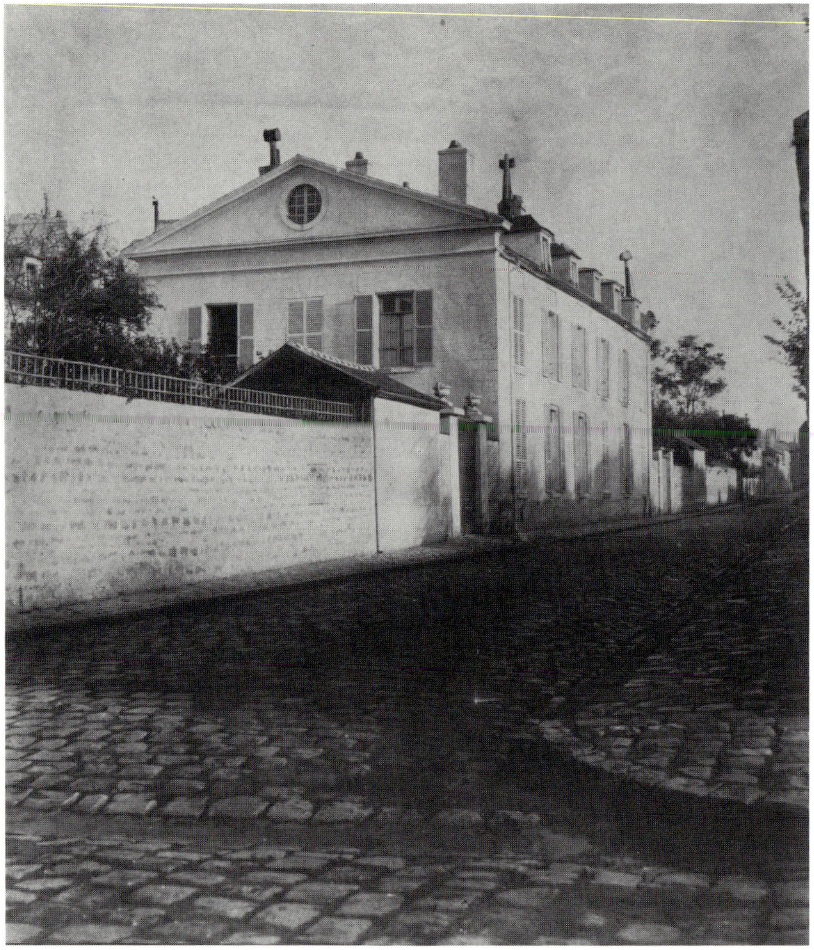

66. LEON TRIPIER
The Author's House

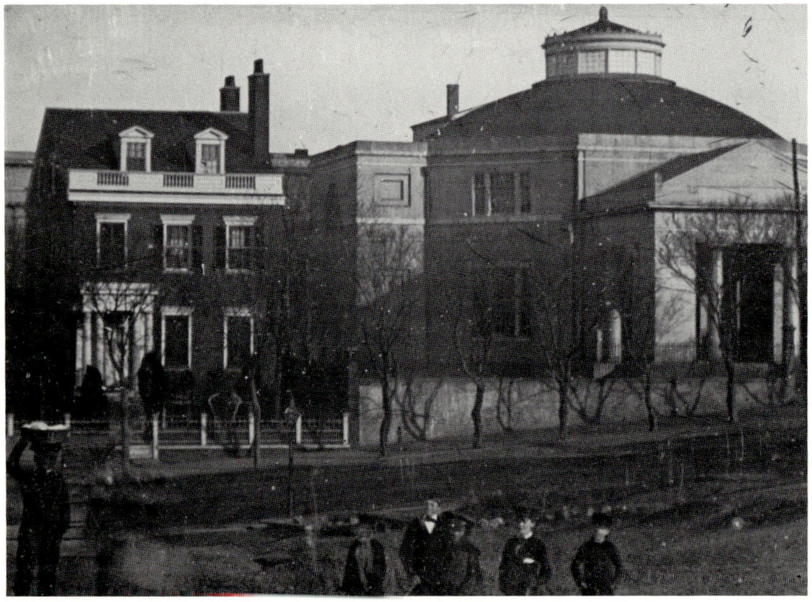

67. UNIDENTIFIED PHOTOGRAPHER
Monumental Church, Richmond, Virginia

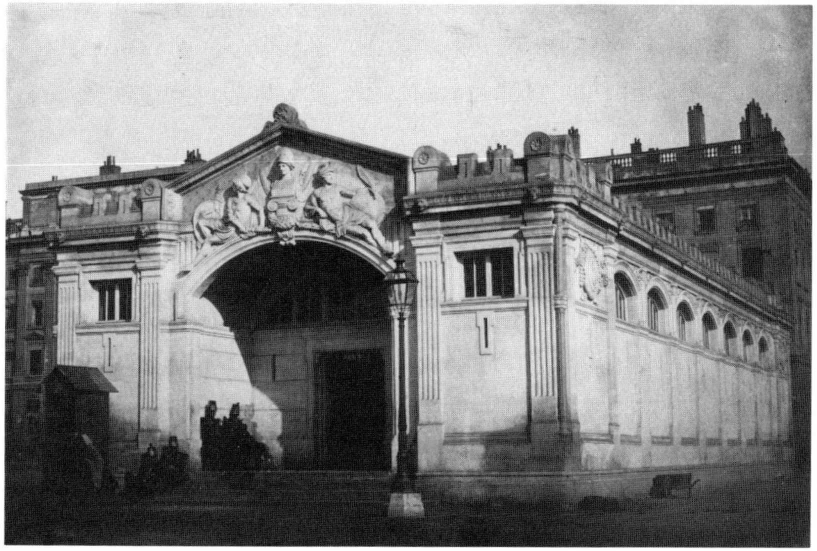

68. UNIDENTIFIED PHOTOGRAPHER
Guard House, Place Bellecour, Lyons

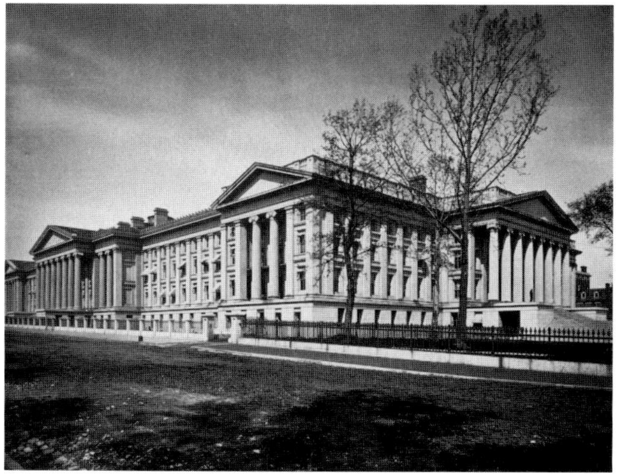

69. UNIDENTIFIED PHOTOGRAPHER
United States Treasury Building

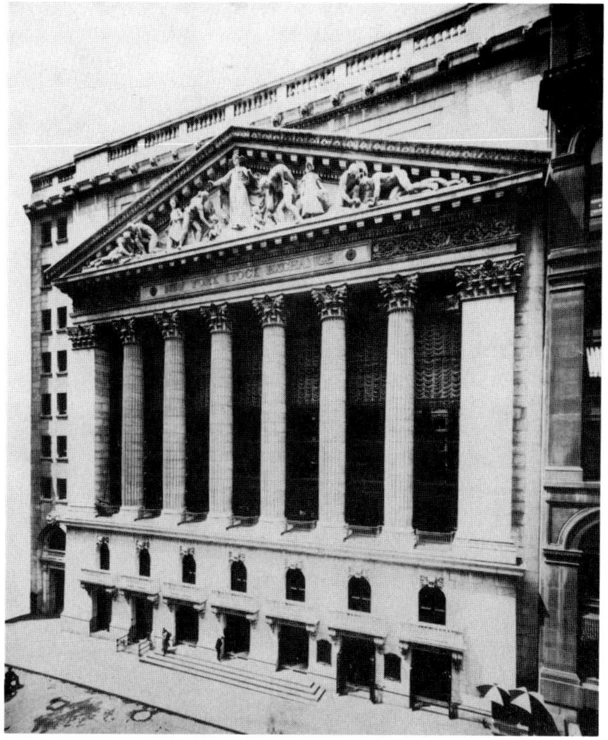

70. UNIDENTIFIED PHOTOGRAPHER
New York Stock Exchange

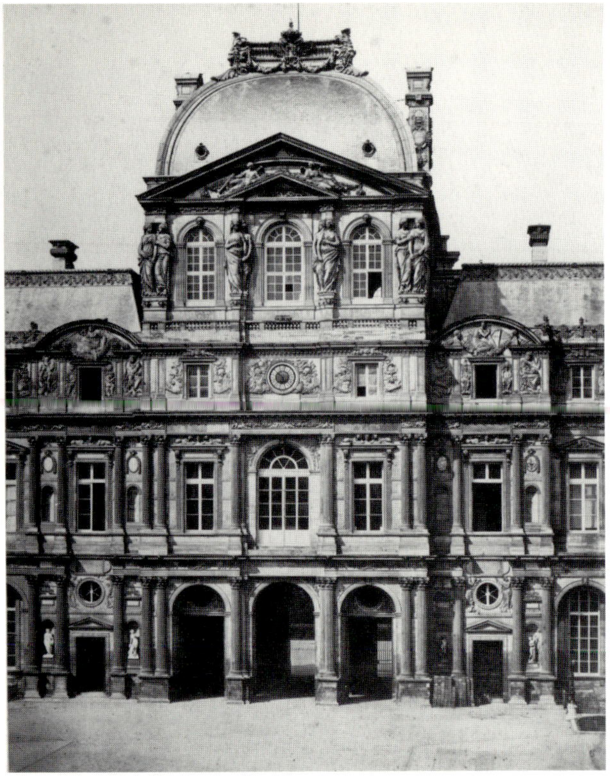

71. EDOUARD-DENIS BALDUS
The New Louvre: Pavillon d'Horloge

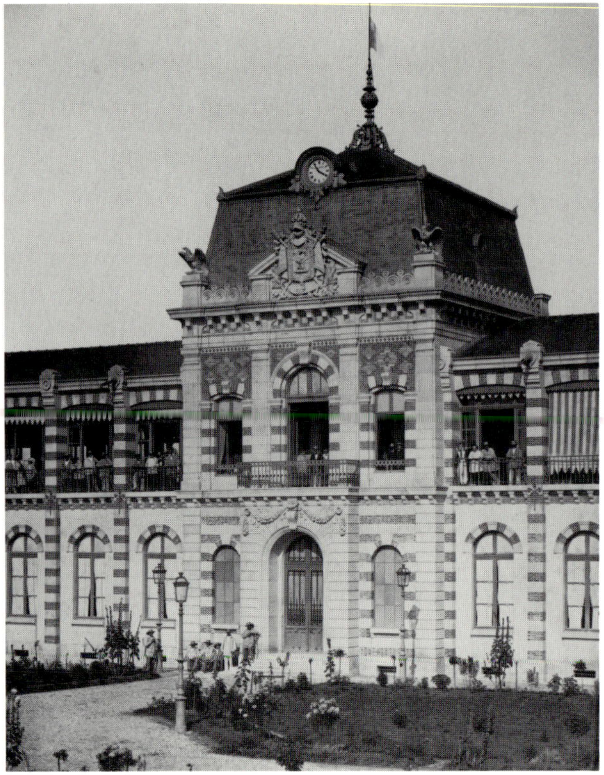

73. CHARLES NEGRE
Imperial Asylum at Vincennes

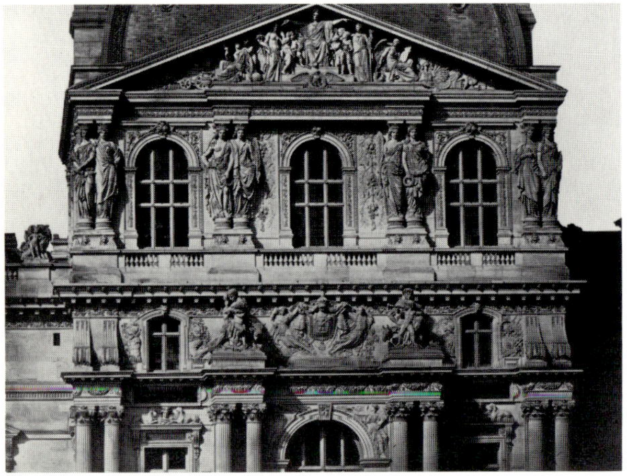

72. EDOUARD-DENIS BALDUS
The New Louvre: Pavillon Richelieu (Detail)

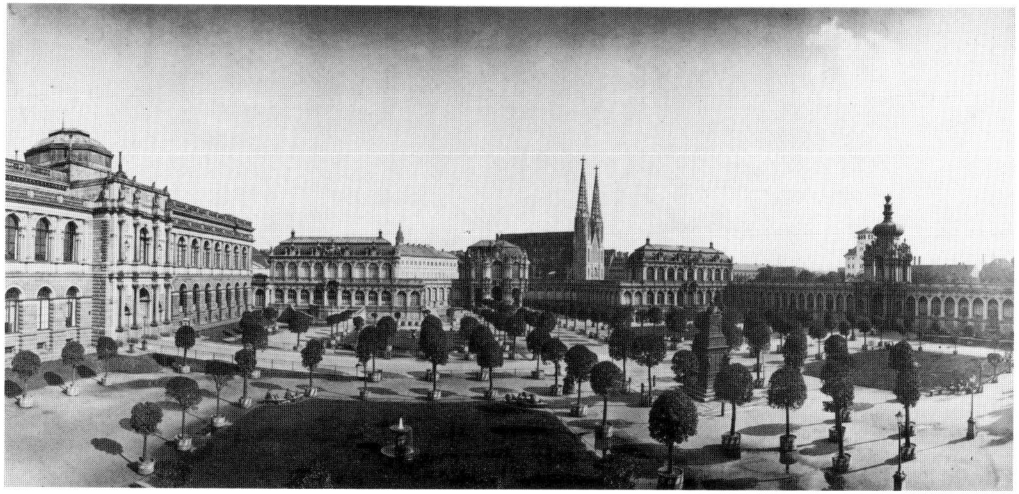

74. UNIDENTIFIED PHOTOGRAPHER
The Zwinger, Interior Courtyard, Dresden

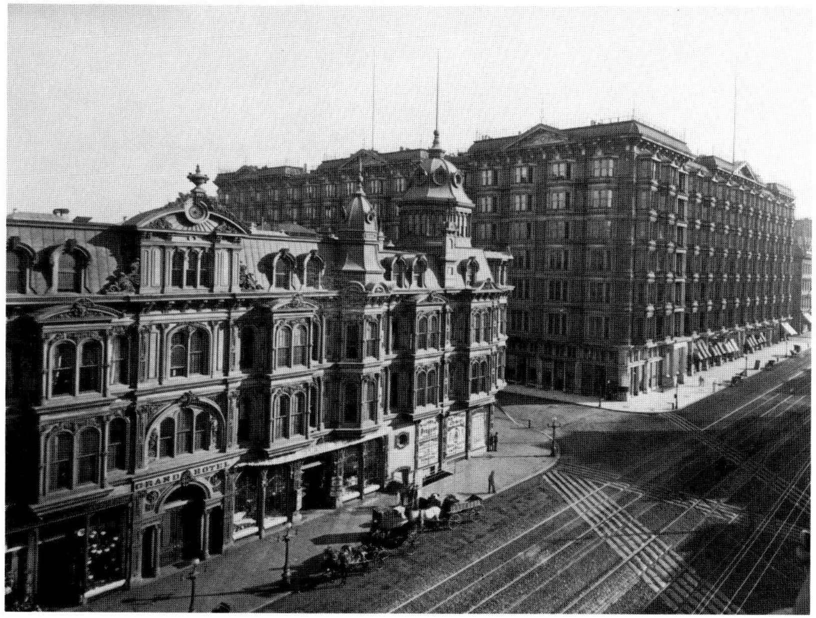

75. ISAIAH WEST TABER
Grand and Palace Hotels, San Francisco, Cal.

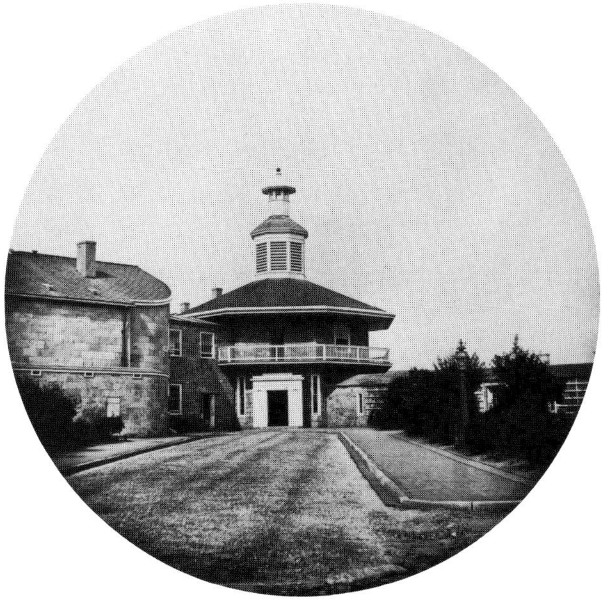

76. (JOSIAH JOHNSON HAWES)
Octagonal Building, Boston (?)

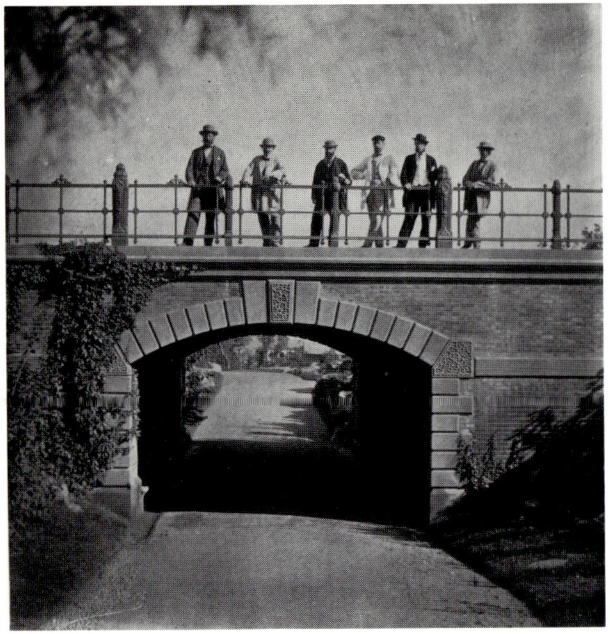

77. VICTOR PREVOST
Bridge No. 3, September 23

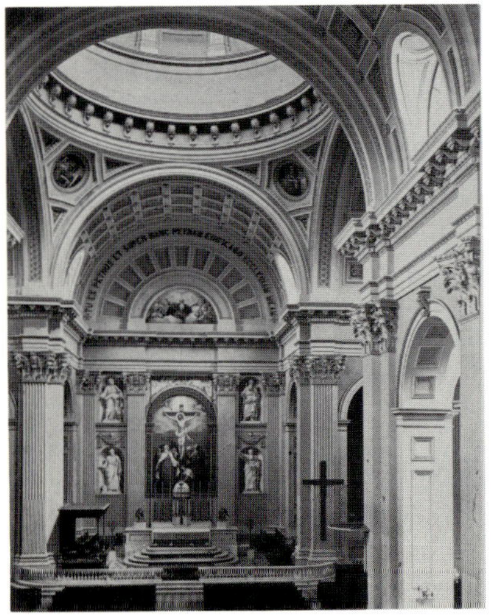

78. FREDERICK GUTEKUNST
Sanctuary & Grand Altar of the Cathedral of St. Peter & St. Paul, Philadelphia

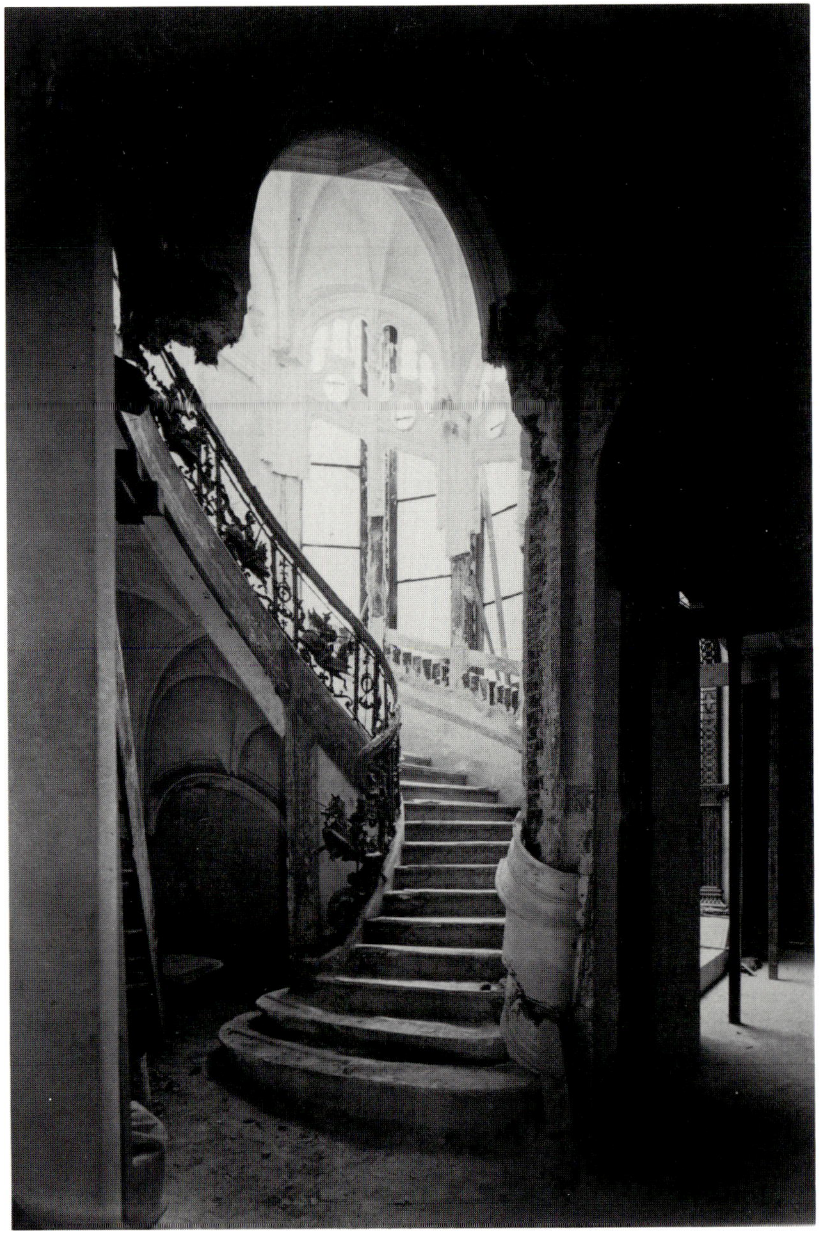

79. (HYACINTHE CESAR or CLEMENCE JACOB DELMAET and LOUIS-EMILE DURANDELLE)
Stairwell Interior in Ruins

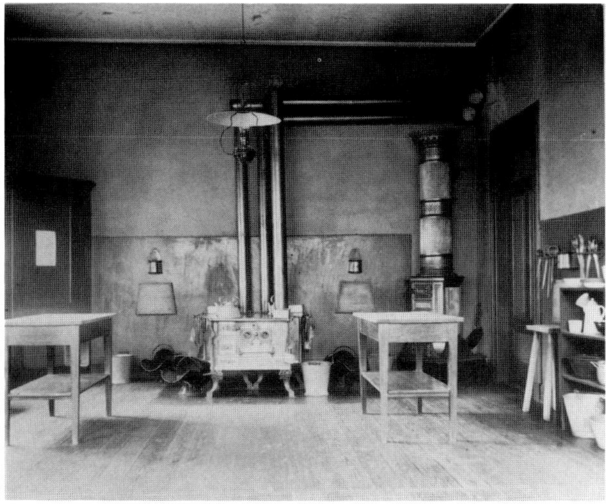

80. UNIDENTIFIED PHOTOGRAPHER
Kitchen of the Home Economics School for Poor Young Women in Kiel

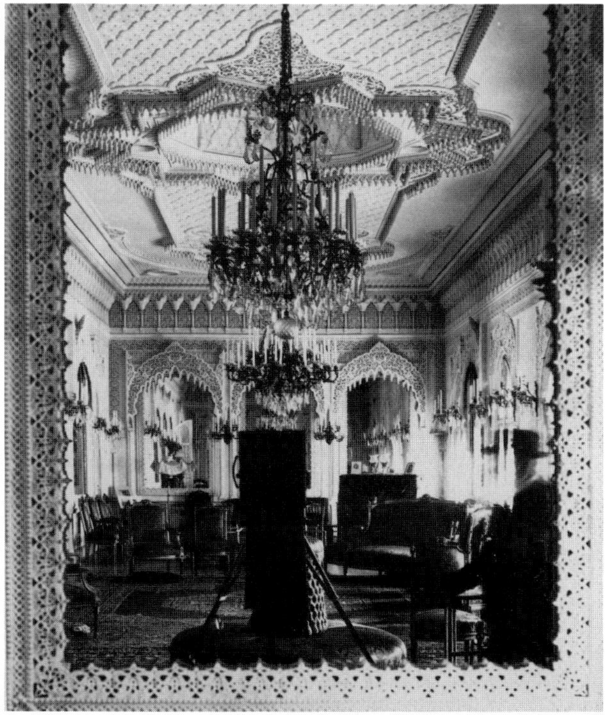

81. LOUIS-ALPHONSE DAVANNE
The Governor's Salon, Algiers, Mirror Effect

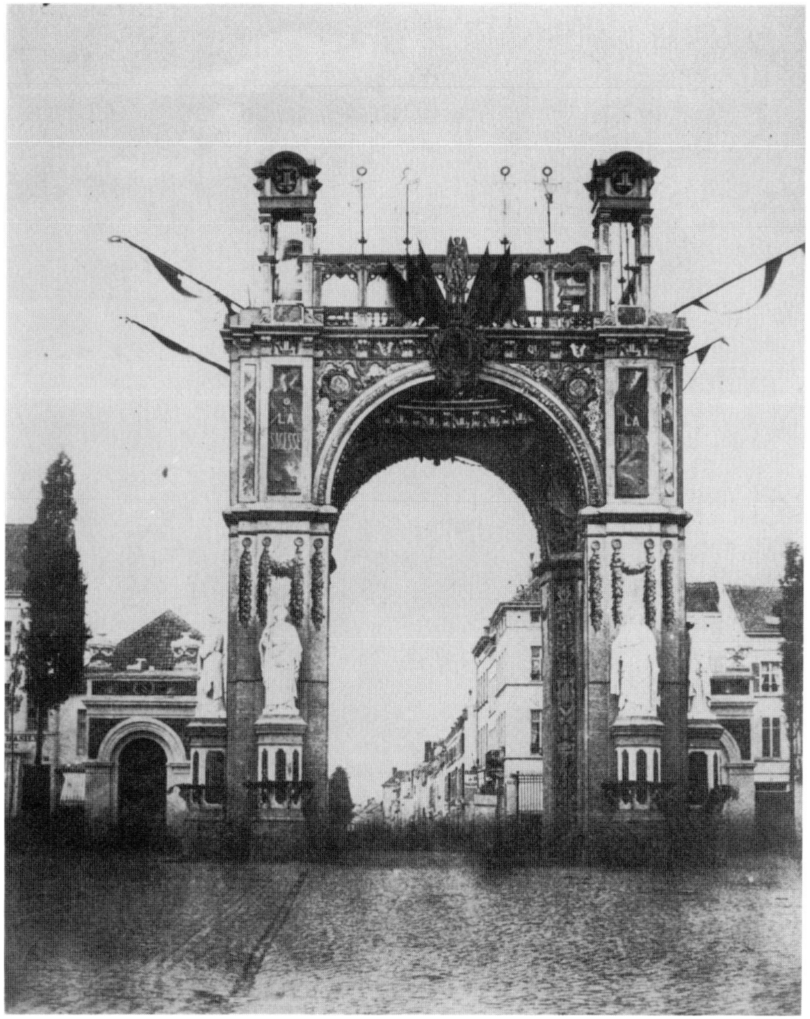

82. (LOUIS-DESIRE BLANQUART-EVRARD)
Triumphal Arch, Belgium, to Commemorate the Reign of Leopold I

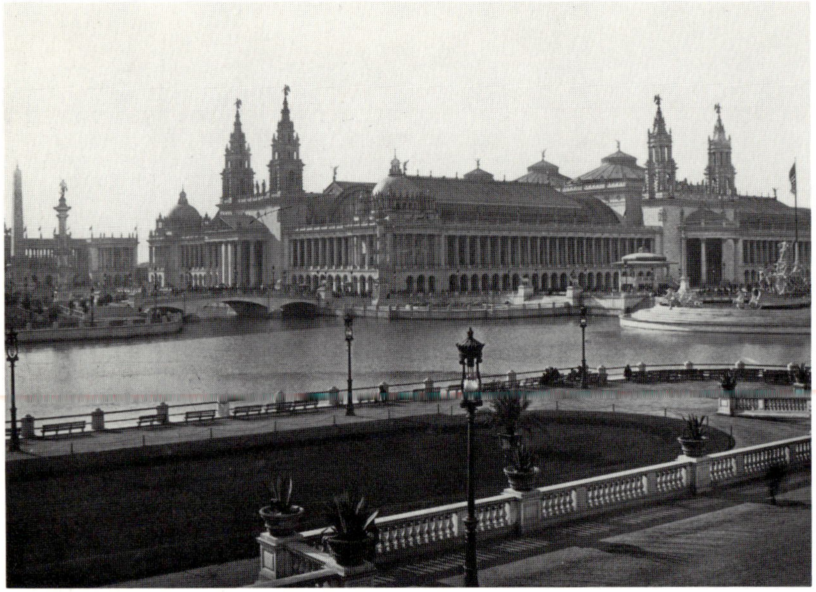

83. UNIDENTIFIED PHOTOGRAPHER
Machinery Hall, View from the Southwest

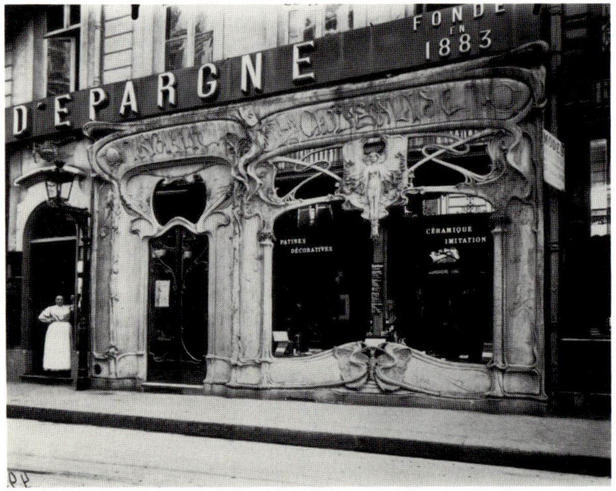

84. JEAN-EUGENE-AUGUSTE ATGET
Art Nouveau Store, 45 rue St. Augustin, Paris

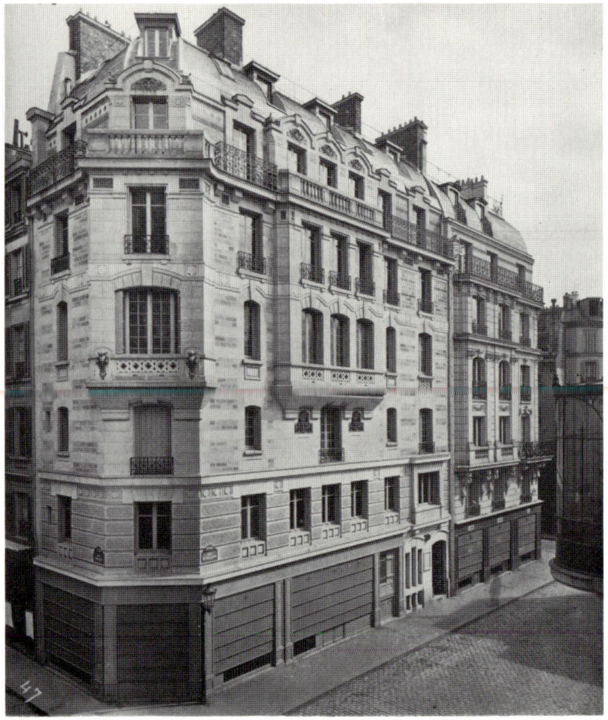

85. ALBERT LEVY
Apartment Building, Corner of Rue de Mogador and Rue Joubert, Paris, 9th Arrondisement

IV. THE RUSTIC AND THE VERNACULAR

"Before God there are neither good nor bad architects. . . . In towns, in the realms of Beelzebub, there may be fine distinctions, as there are even in kinds of crime. And I therefore ask: why is it that every architect, whether he is good or bad, harms the lakeside? The peasant does not. . . . The peasant wanted to build a house for himself, his kin and his cattle, and he has succeeded. As his neighbor and his ancestor succeeded. As the animal succeeds, guided by its instincts. Is the house beautiful? Yes, just as beautiful as the rose and the thistle, the horse and the cow. I therefore ask again: why does the architect, be he a good one or a bad one, harm the lakeside? Because the architect, like practically every townsman, has no culture. He lacks the security of the peasant, who does have a culture. . . . I call culture that harmony between the inner and the outer man which alone guarantees sensible thinking and acting."—(Adolf Loos [architect], 1909)

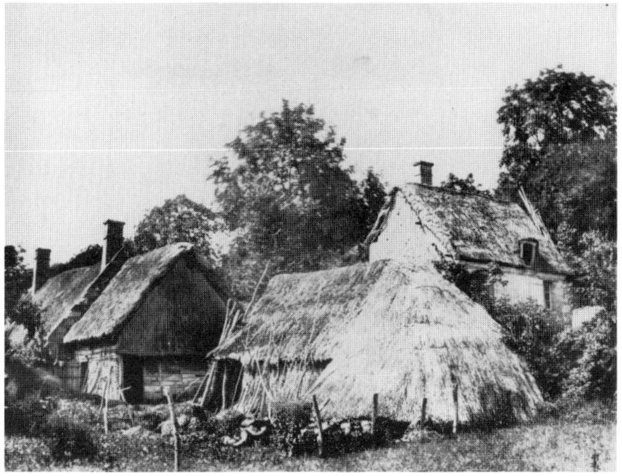

86. VICTOR PREVOST
Corner of a Farm

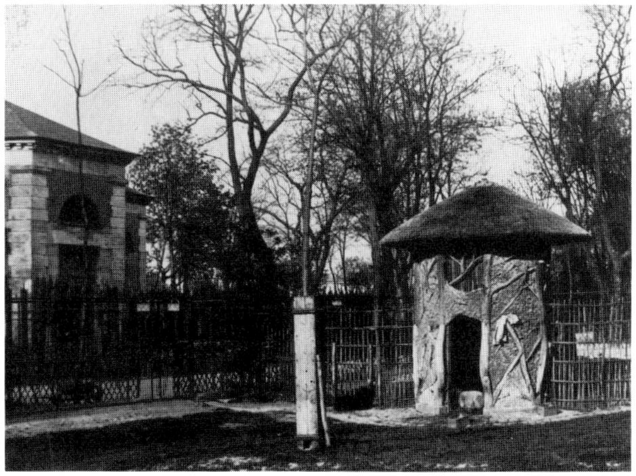

87. (CHARLES MARVILLE)
Lamb Shed at the Jardin des Plantes, Paris

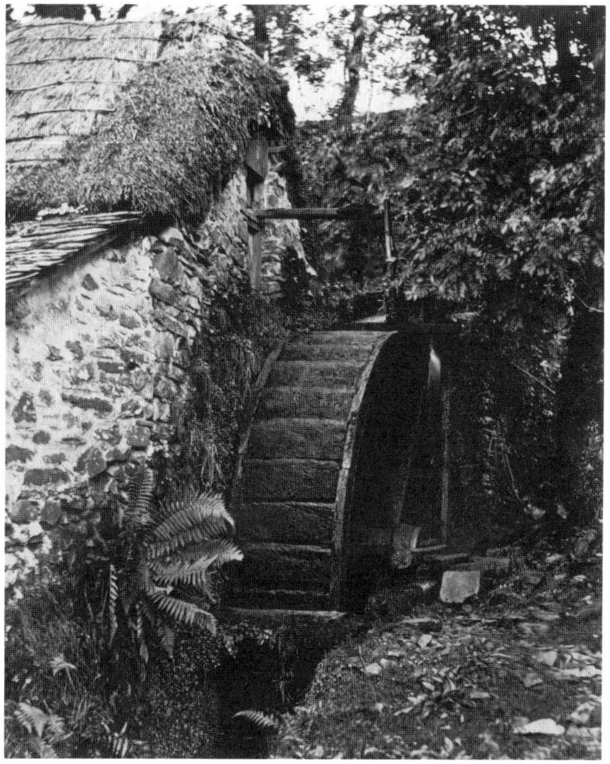

88. JOHN PERCY and JOHN SPILLER
The New Mill, Near Lynton, North Devon

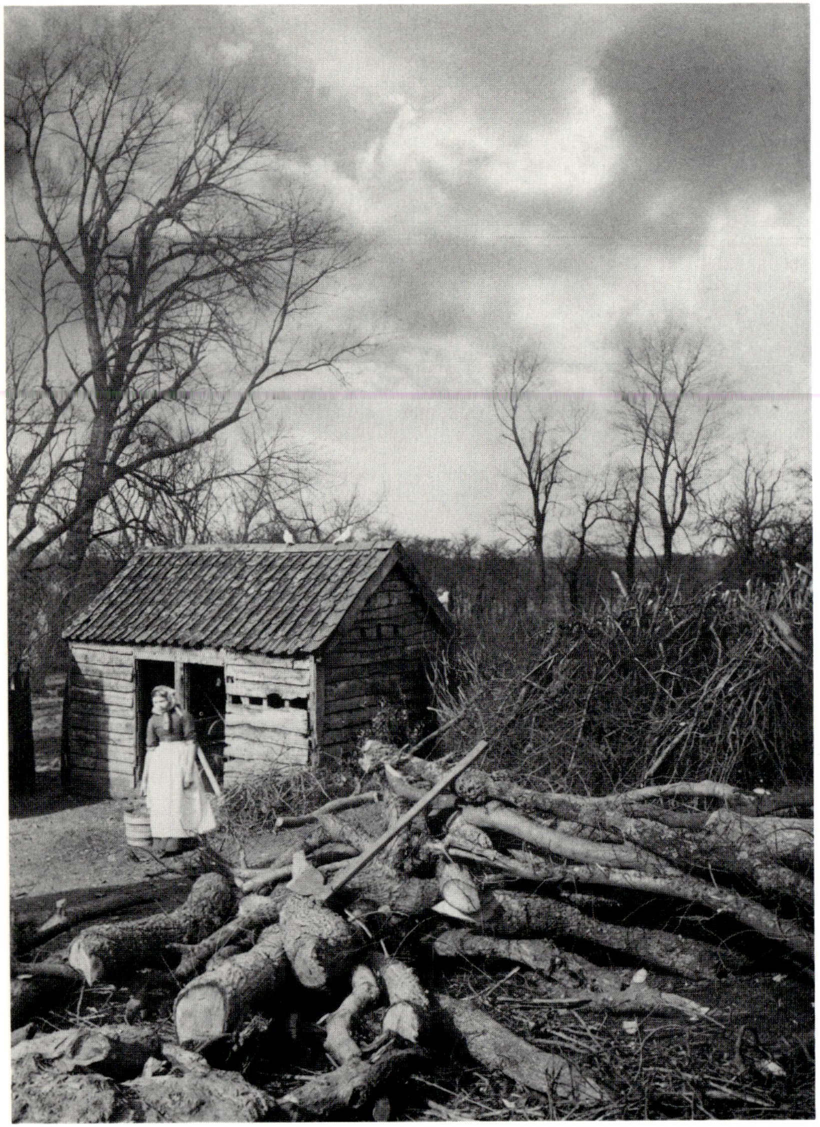

89. PETER HENRY EMERSON
Farm Scene, Woman Carrying Bucket

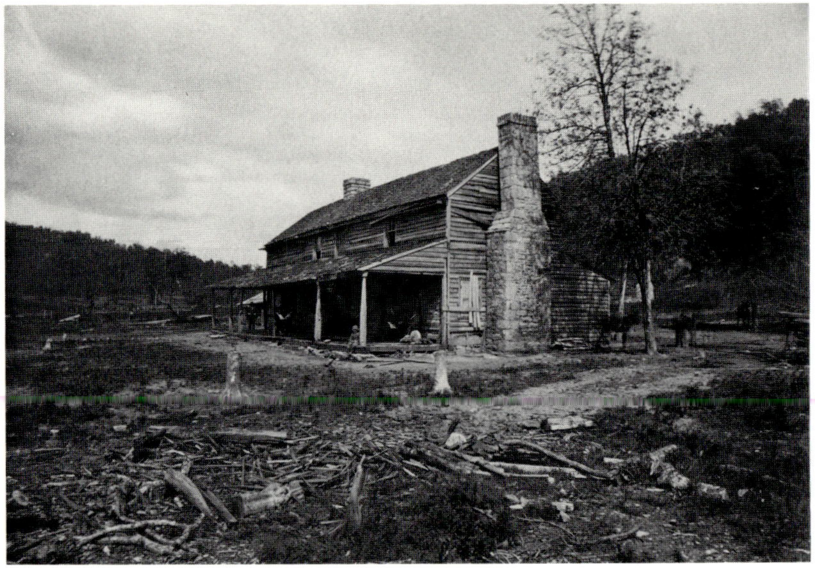

90. GEORGE N. BARNARD
The John Ross House, Ringold, Georgia

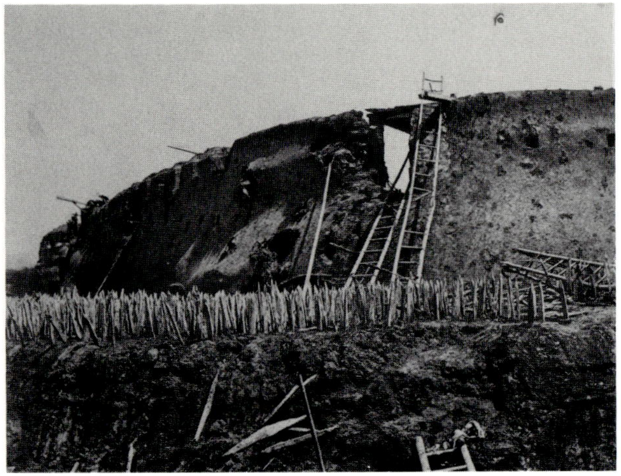

91. FELICE BEATO
Exterior of Fort Taku, Northern China, Showing French Entrance

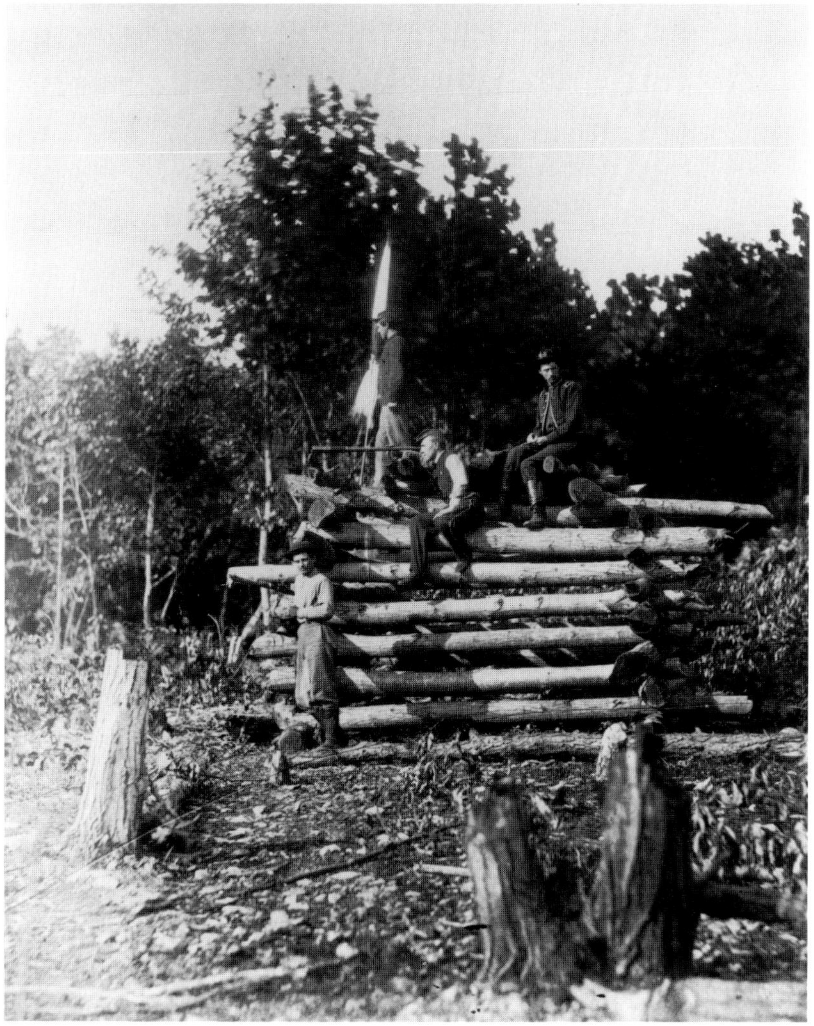

92. TIMOTHY O'SULLIVAN
Signal Tower on Elk Mountain, Maryland, Overlooking Battlefield of Antietam

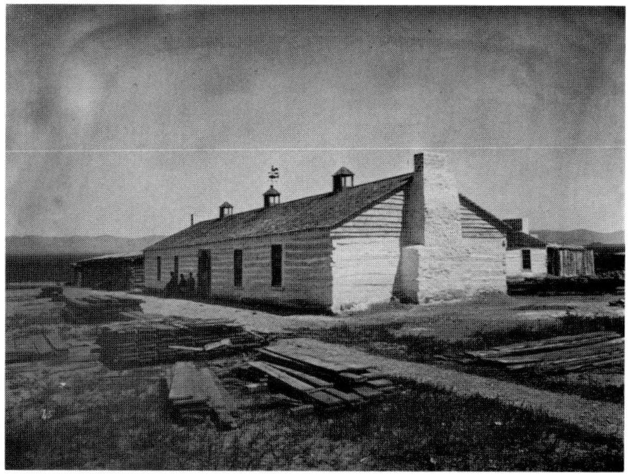

93. TIMOTHY O'SULLIVAN
Camp Ruby, Ruby Valley, Nevada

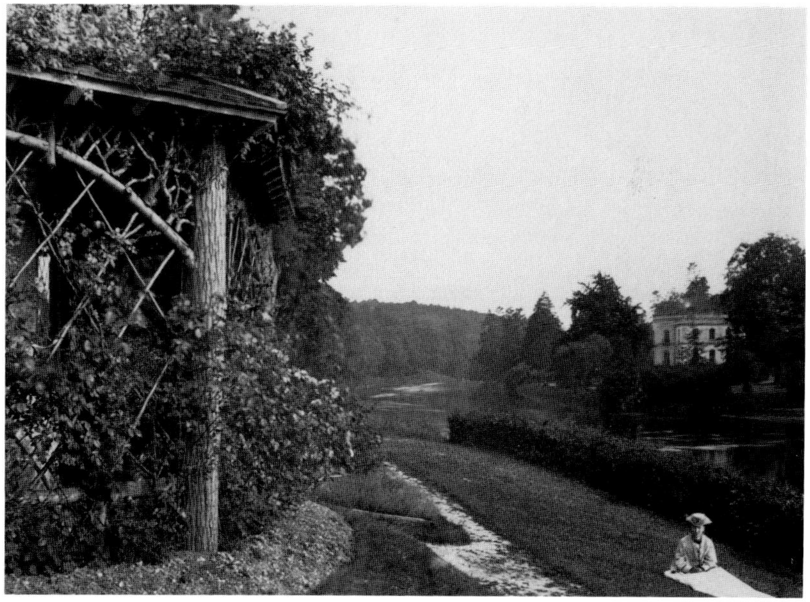

94. JOHN HYDE
A Porch in Chiefden Woods

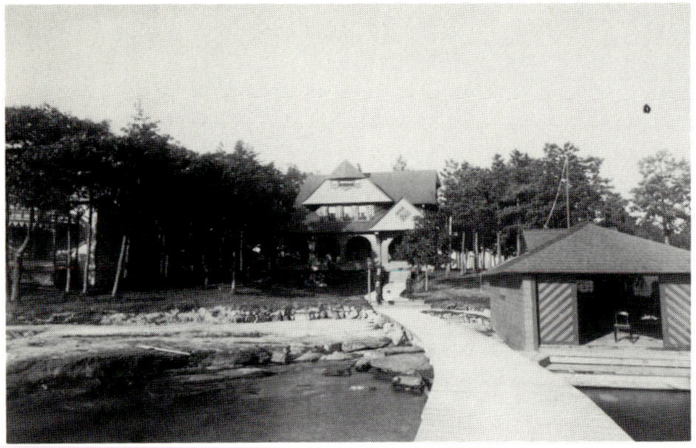

95. UNIDENTIFIED PHOTOGRAPHER
House and Boat House, View from the Dock

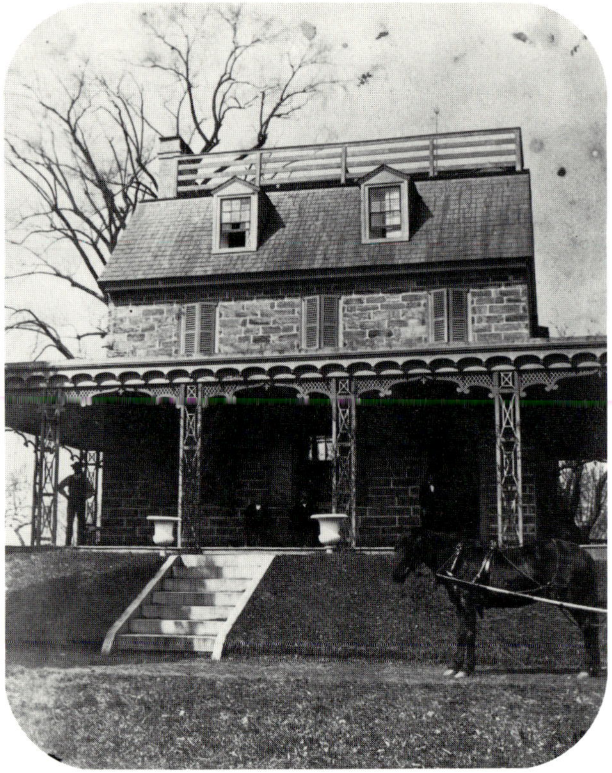

96. FREDERICK DEBOURG RICHARDS
John McAllister's House

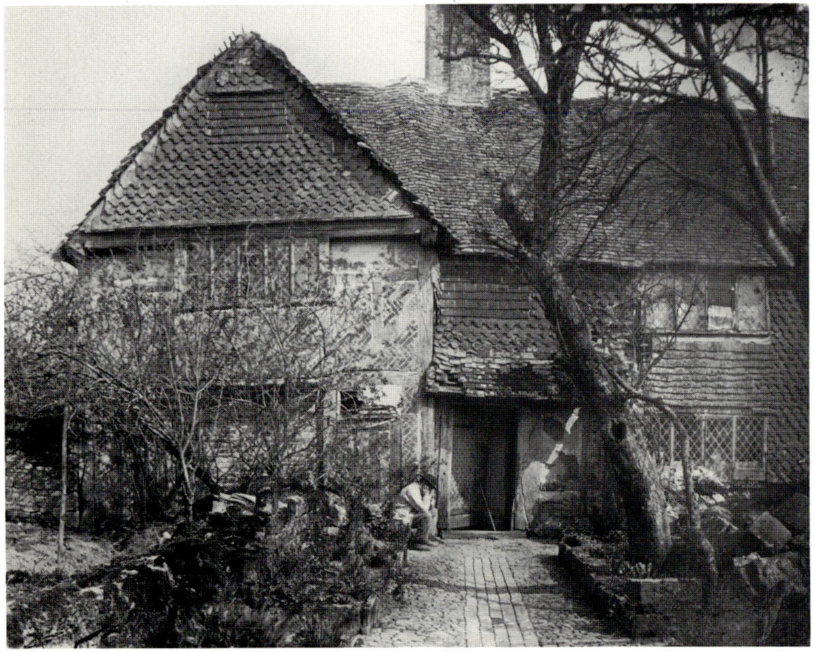

97. UNIDENTIFIED PHOTOGRAPHER
Rural Cottage, Half-Timbered Construction

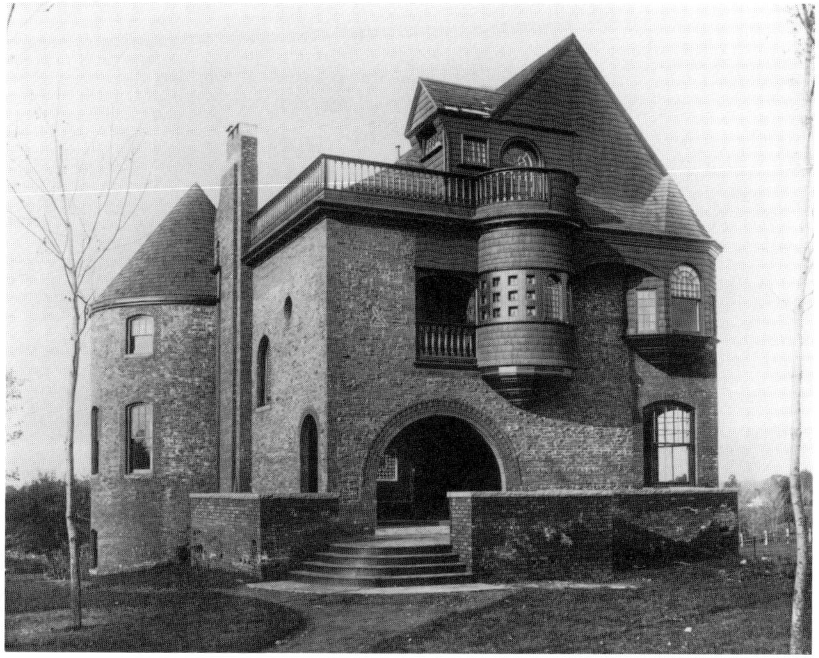

98. UNIDENTIFIED PHOTOGRAPHER
Residence of Mr. C. S. French, Newport, Rhode Island

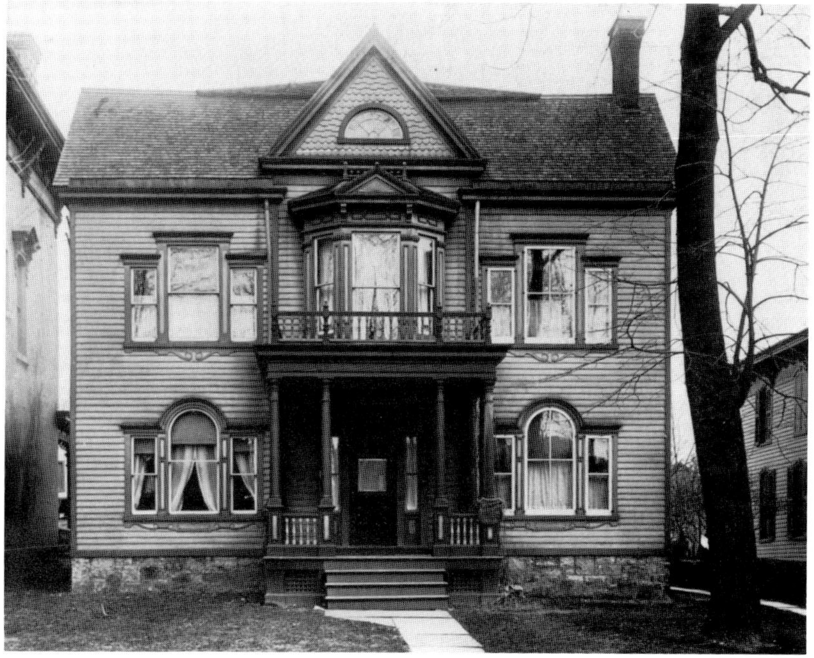

99. UNIDENTIFIED PHOTOGRAPHER
Mrs. Deecke's Kindergarten and Graded School

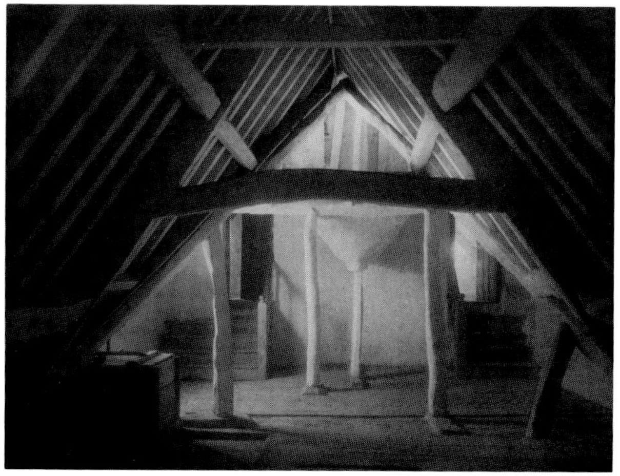

100. FREDERICK H. EVANS
Kelmscott Manor, Attics

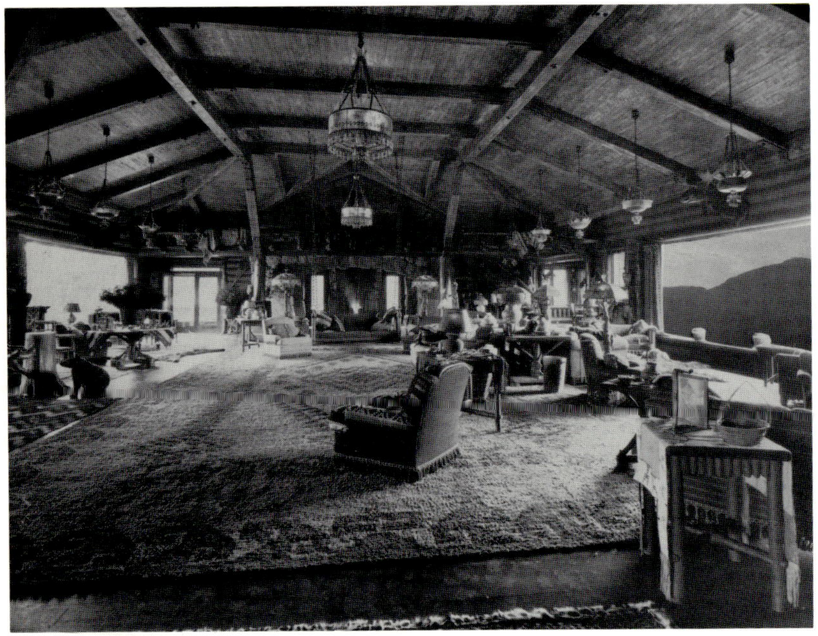

101. UNIDENTIFIED PHOTOGRAPHER
Mr. E. F. Hutton's "Camp Hutridge," The Indian Room

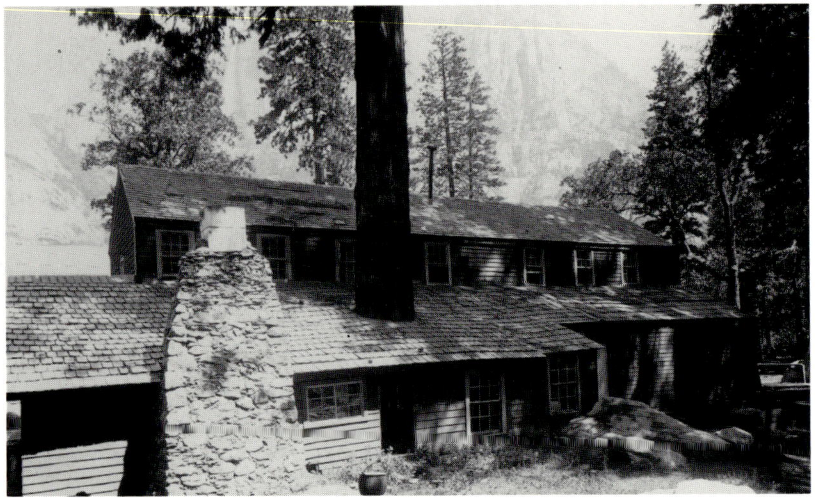

102. ISAIAH WEST TABER
Barnard's Hotel, Yosemite Valley, California

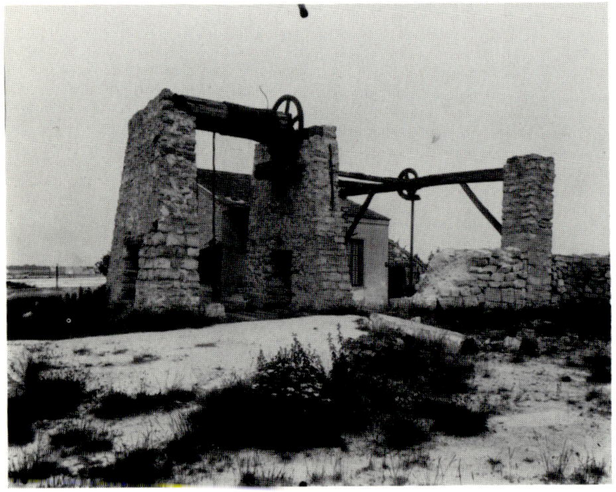

103. JEAN-EUGENE-AUGUSTE ATGET
Bagneux: Old Quarry Wells

V. CONSTRUCTION AND PROGRESS

"I wish to speak about engineers. The distinction between architect and engineer is a rather modern one. It takes a portion of a whole and makes it a specialty; it divides an art into two parts, and one of them it makes a distinct profession. . . . what is the practical result of this division? . . . The engineers are given work that demands carefulness, skill, science, and even more; but when one thinks art alone is at stake, their services are renounced in favor of the architects. This is an irrationality that cannot be explained, a strange misinterpretation of the art of building. Who can really demarcate? Where does art begin? Where does it end? The bridge, the viaduct, even the roundhouse can be as artistic as the railway terminal, and architecture can be manifested in a cabin as well as a palace."—(Charles Garnier [architect], 1869)

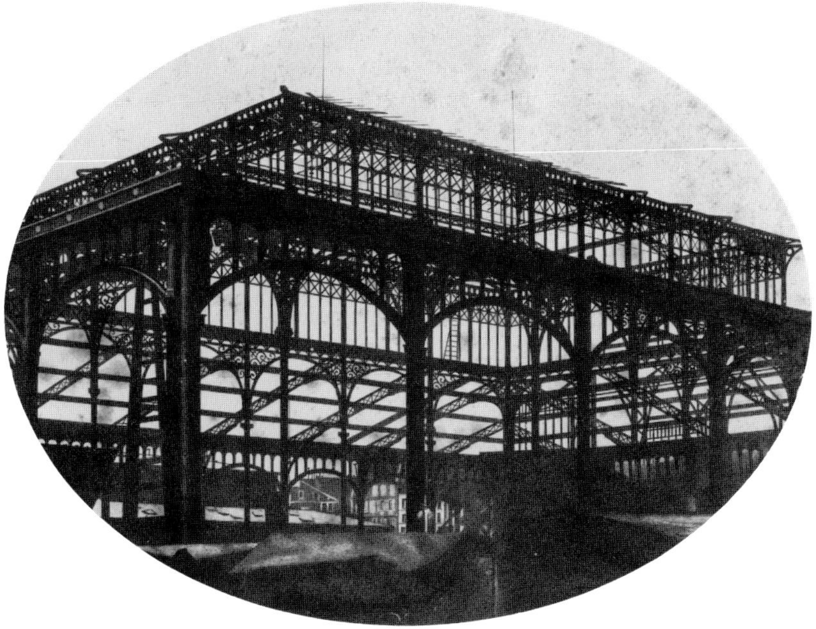

104. UNIDENTIFIED PHOTOGRAPHER
Halles Centrales, Paris. View of the Southwestern Pavilion During Construction

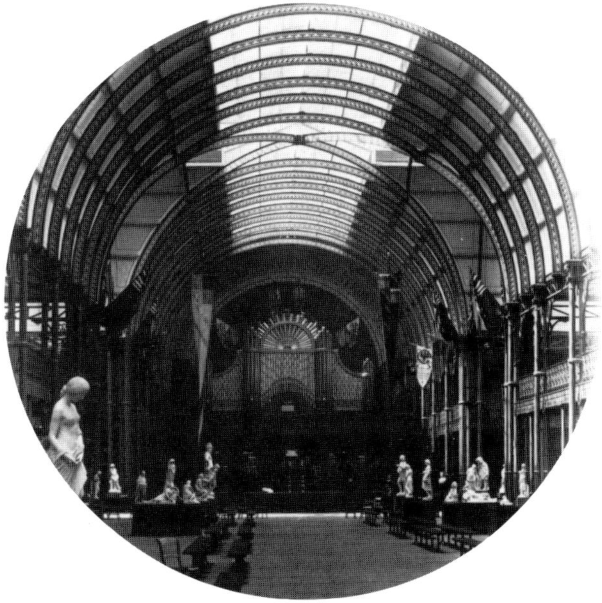

105. PHILIP HENRY DELAMOTTE
View in Central Hall, Art Treasures Exhibition, Manchester

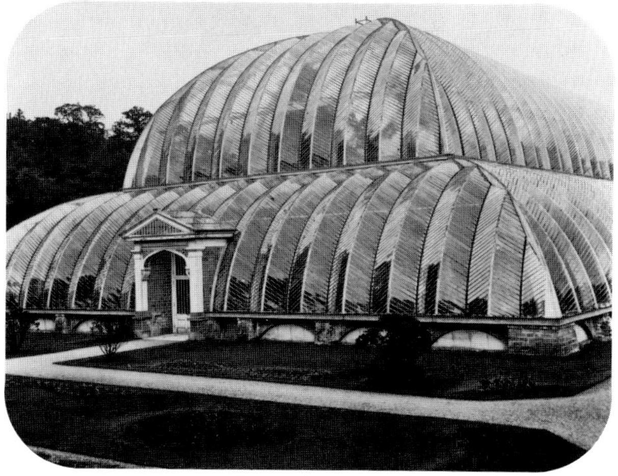

106. J. A. WARWICK
The Conservatory

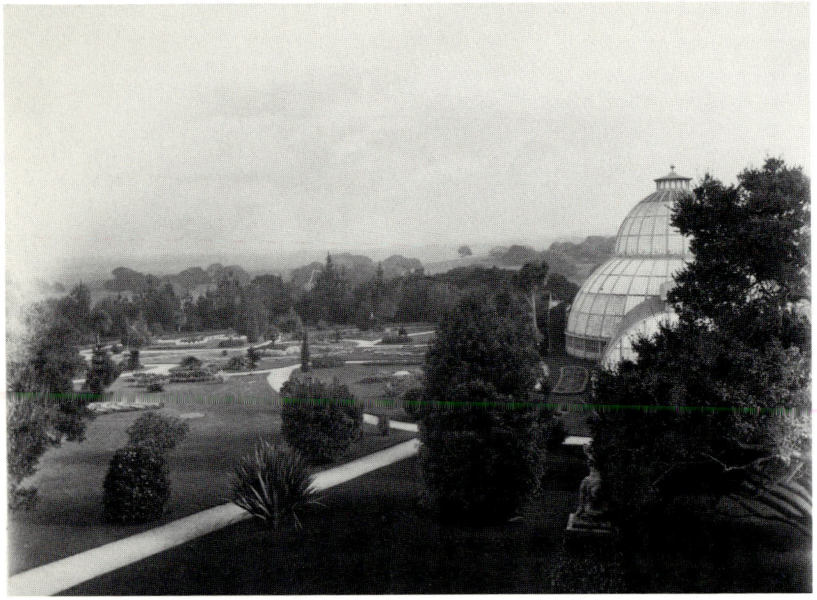

107. ISAIAH WEST TABER
Mr. D. O. Mills' Residence at Millbrae, Cal., View Near the Conservatory

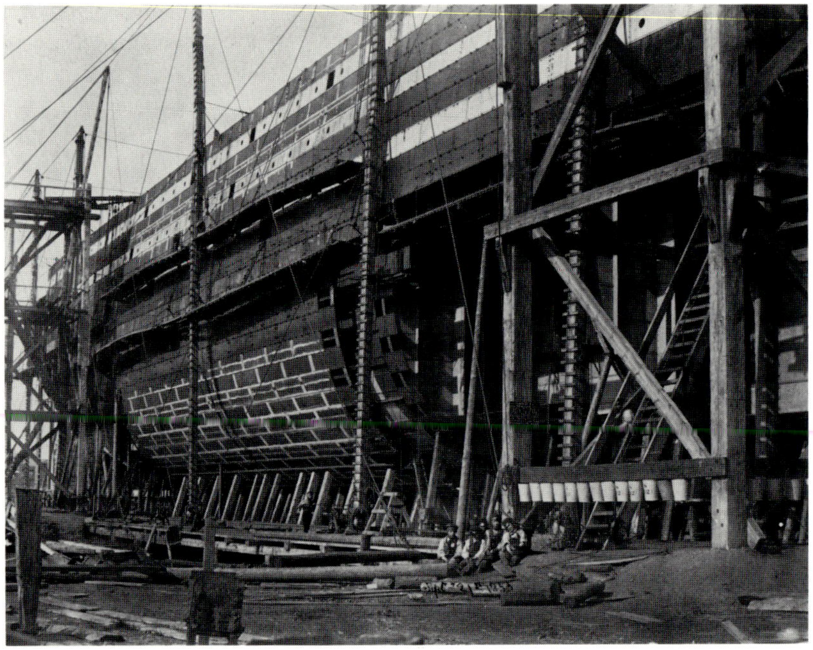

108. JOSEPH CUNDALL
The "Leviathan" During Its Construction. Sept. 21, 1855

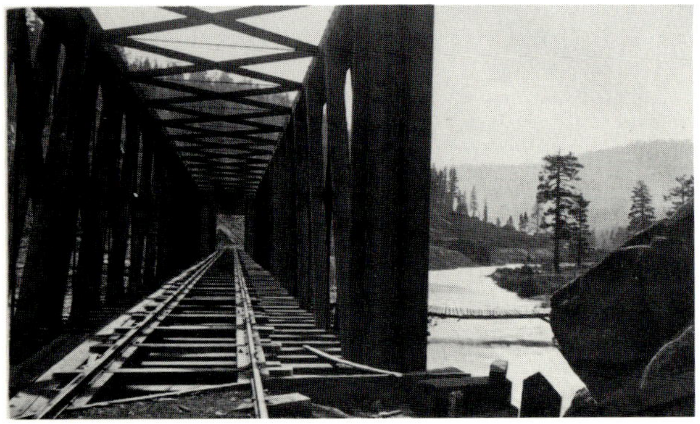

109. CLARENCE LEANDER WEED
Pacific Coast Scenery: Bridge at the Second Crossing of the Truckee River, Nevada, Central Pacific RR

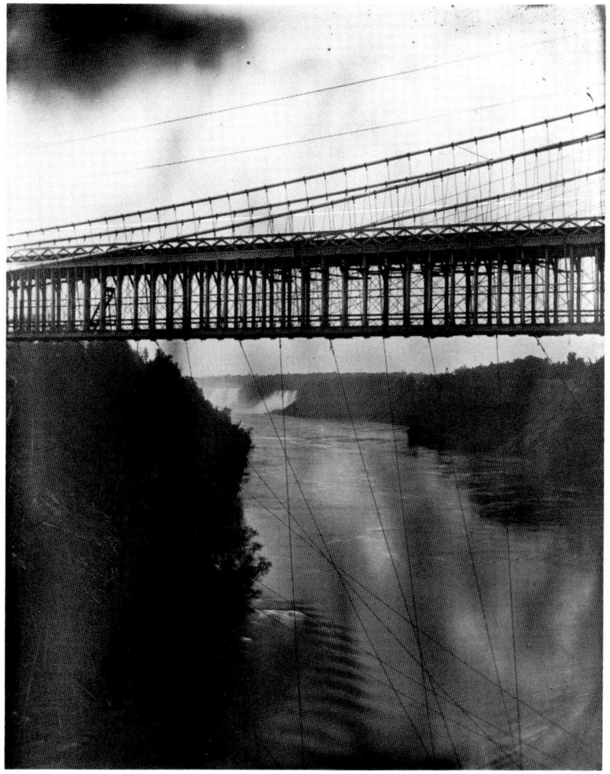

110. ALBERT SANDS SOUTHWORTH and
JOSIAH JOHNSON HAWES
J. A. Roebling's Suspension Bridge over the Niagara Gorge

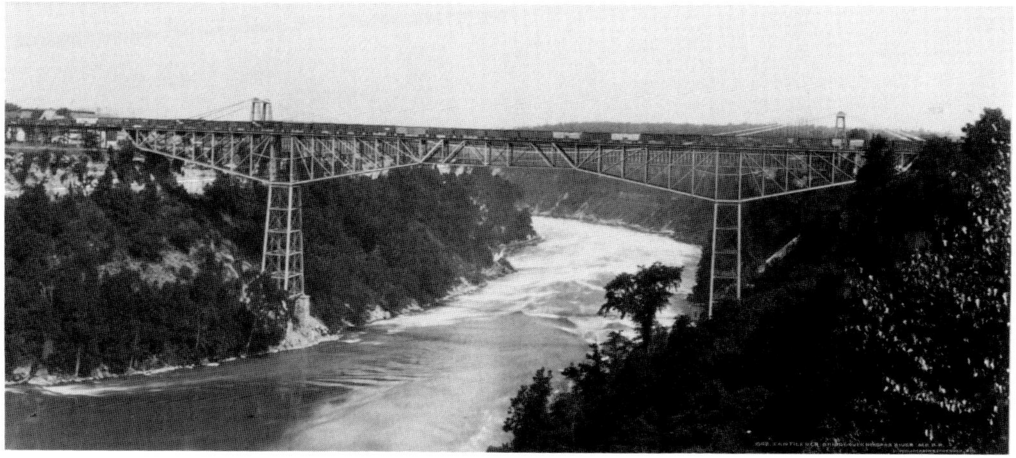

111. WILLIAM HENRY JACKSON
The Cantilever Bridge over Niagara River. M.C.R.R.

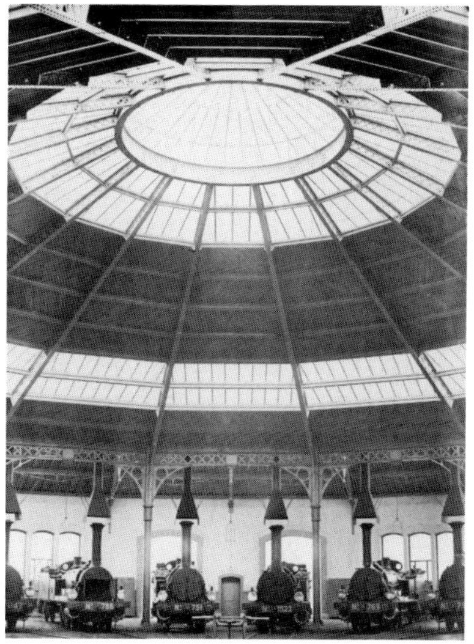

112. A. COLLARD
Roundhouse for 32 Locomotives at Nevers.
First Interior View

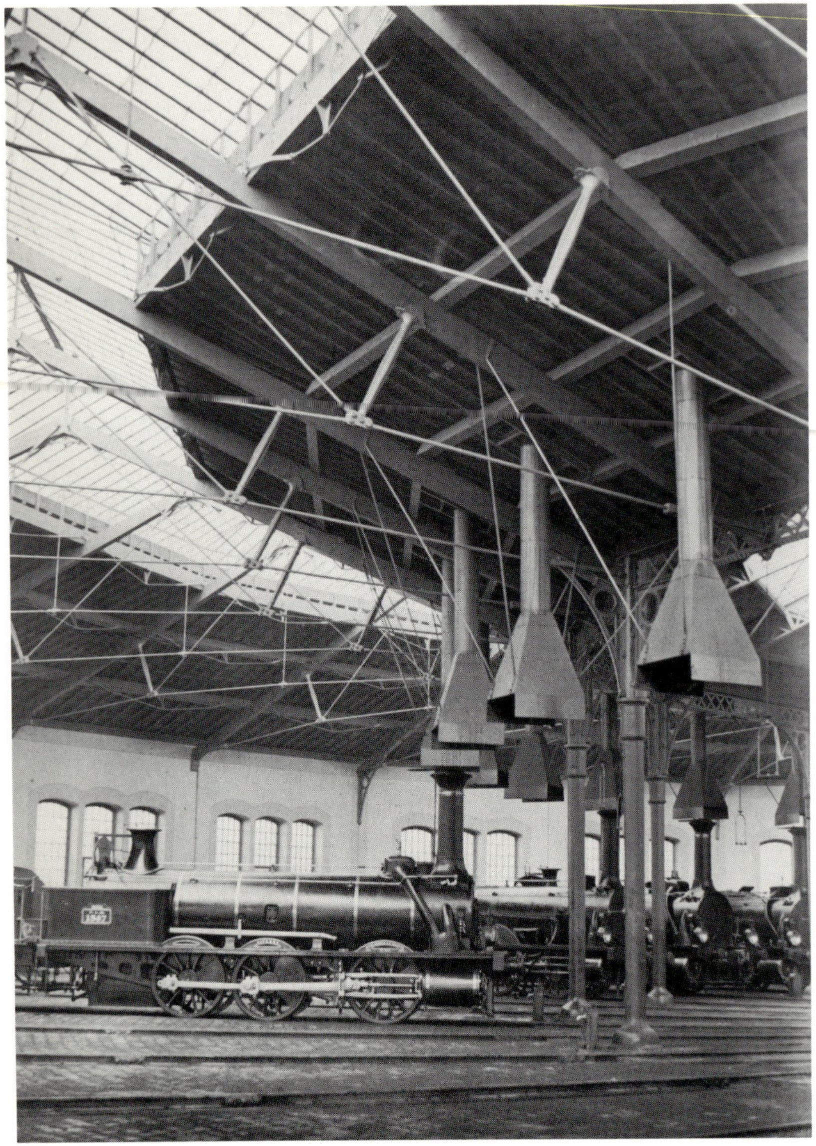

113. A. COLLARD
Roundhouse for 32 Locomotives at Nevers. Third Interior View

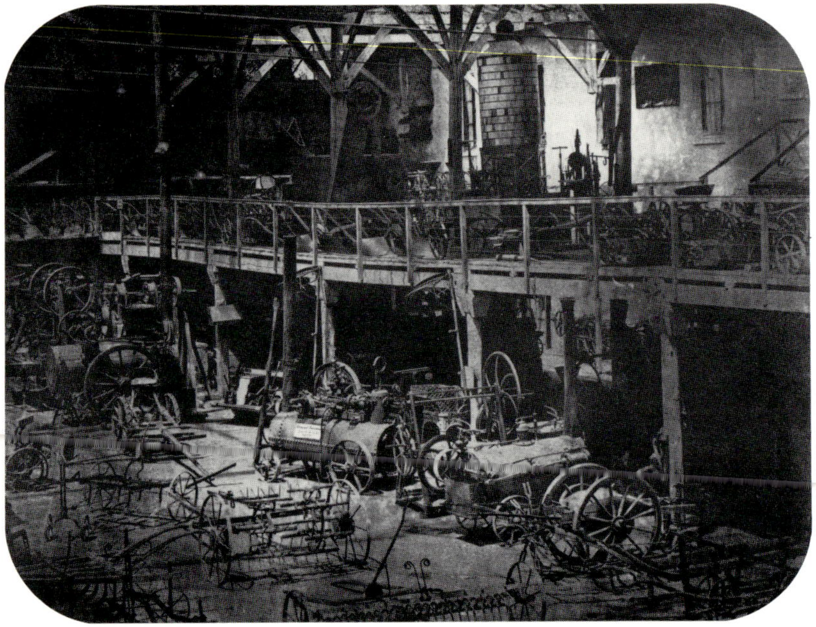

114. PIALLAT
Warehouse of Edmond Ganneron, Specialist in Agricultural Equipment

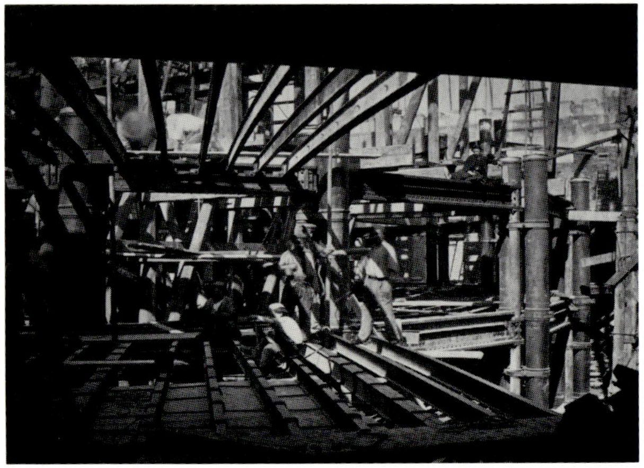

115. HYACINTHE CESAR or CLEMENCE JACOB DELMAET and LOUIS-EMILE DURANDELLE
Interior View of the Construction of Ch. Garnier's Opera House

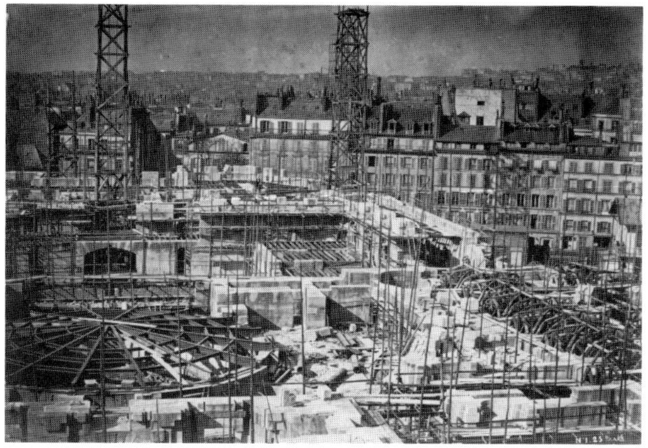

116. HYACINTHE CESAR or CLEMENCE JACOB DELMAET
and LOUIS-EMILE DURANDELLE
View of the Roofs of Ch. Garnier's Opera House Under Construction

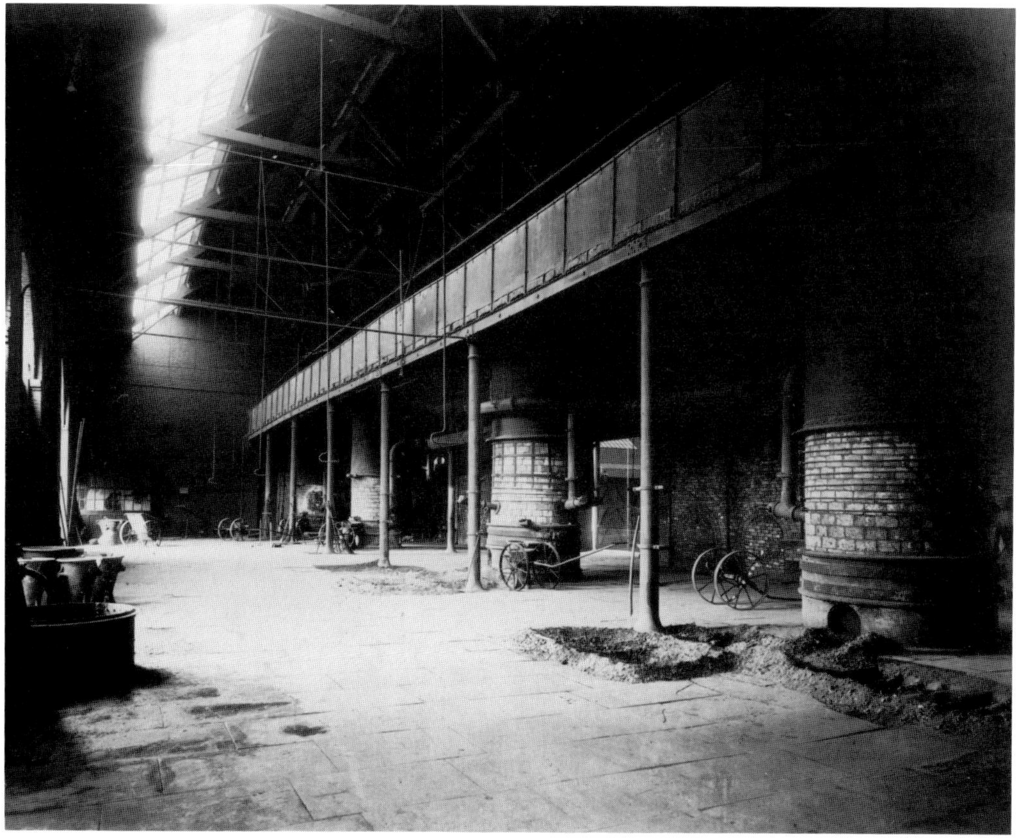

117. LOUIS-EMILE DURANDELLE
Sleeved Industrial Ovens

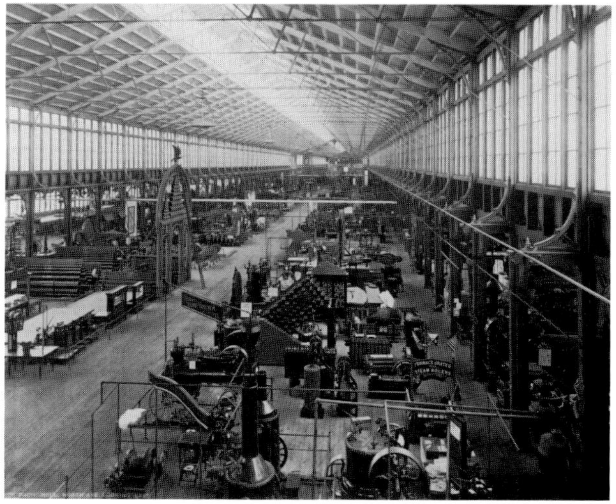

118. CENTENNIAL PHOTOGRAPHIC COMPANY
Machinery Hall, North Ave., Looking East (Centennial Exposition)

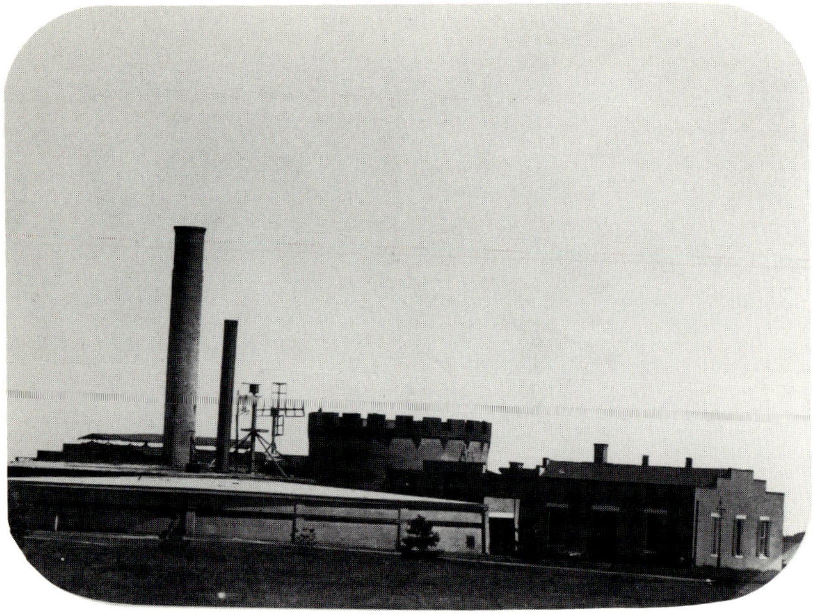

119. FISCHER & BROTHERS
Gas and Steam Works, U.S. Naval Academy

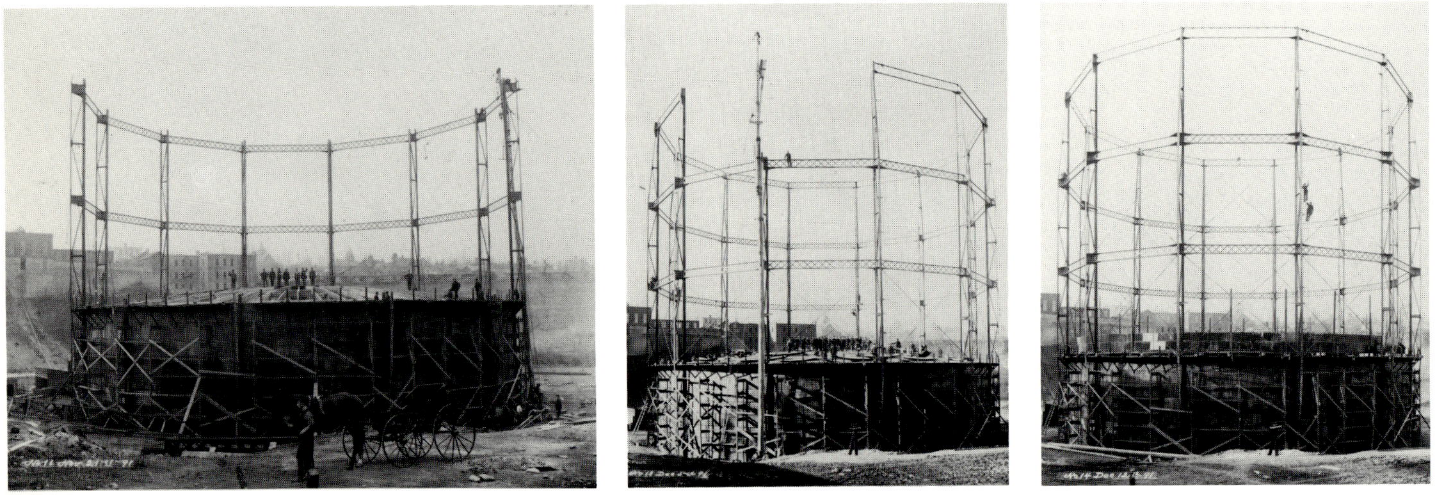

120. UNIDENTIFIED PHOTOGRAPHER
Construction Stages of Storage Tank

VI. OLD CITIES AND NEW

"At one time, we were content to photograph the interiors of cities without trying to introduce daily life into our pictures; on the contrary, we chose the hour when the plazas and streets were deserted and getting rid of a few rare passersby or the curious was not the most agreeable part of the job. It is no longer the same today. Exposure times being reduced from three minutes to less than a second, the photographer can suspend the movements of a great city's active life. Doing so does not require any special manipulations."—(Joseph-Maria Eder [photographer], 1888)

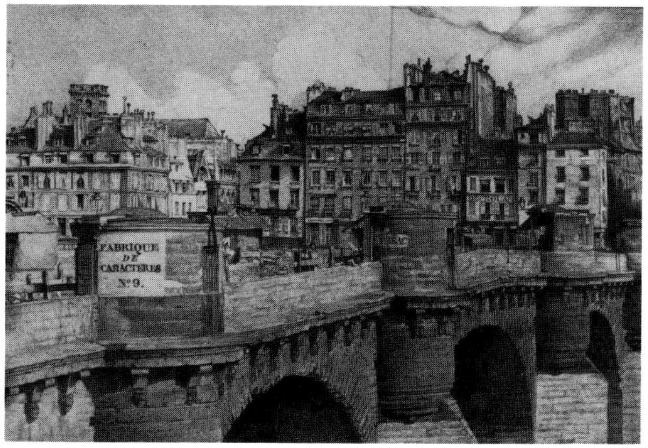

121. (NOEL-MARIE PAYMAL LEREBOURS)
Le Pont Neuf, View Taken from Lerebours Opticians

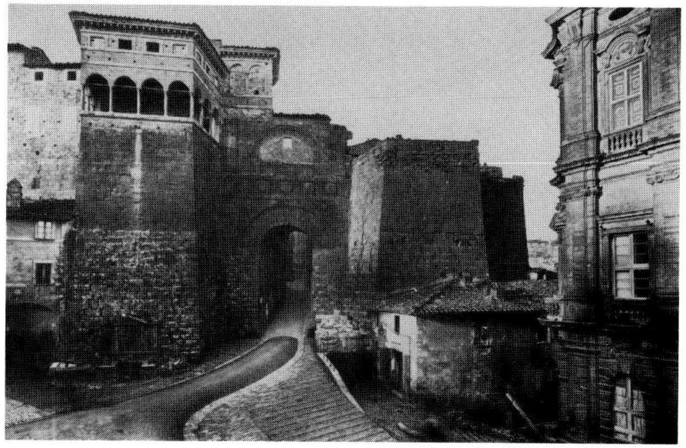

122. ROBERT MACPHERSON
Etruscan Gateway at Perugia

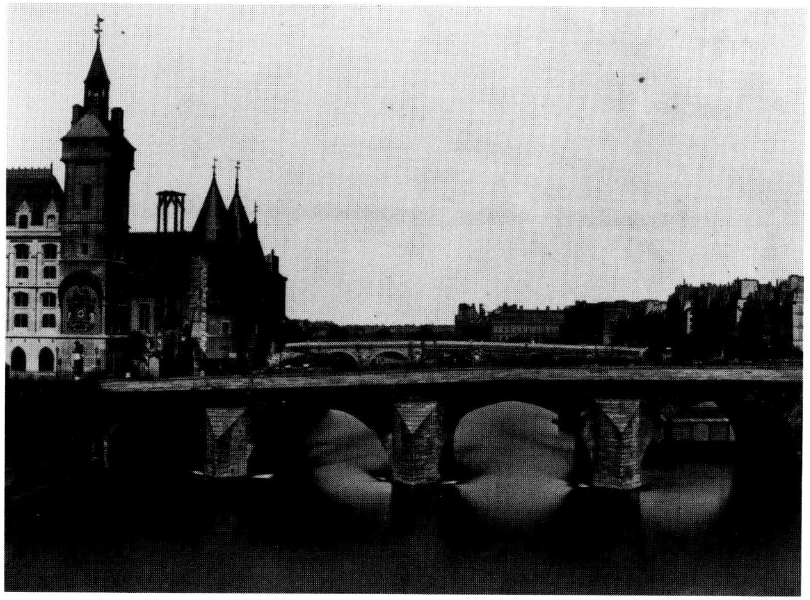

123. FR. ALPH. FORTIER
View Taken from the Pont Notre-Dame, Paris

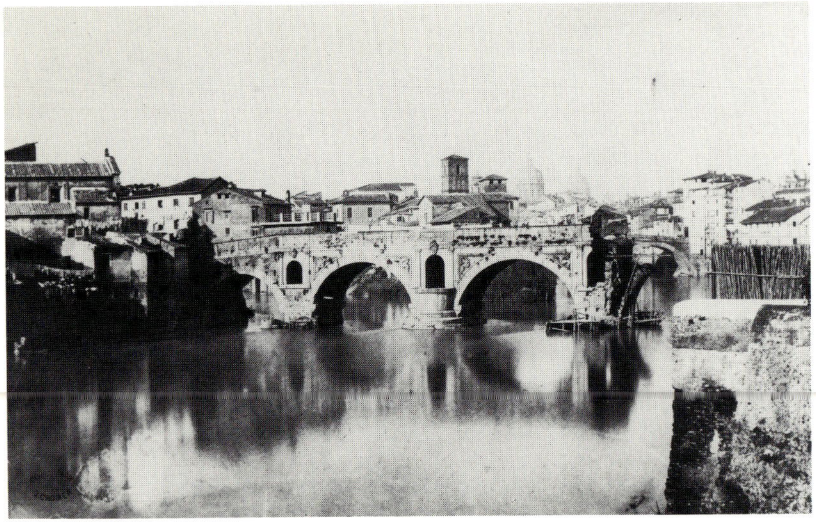

124. (GIACOMO CANEVA)
Ruined Bridge on the Tiber

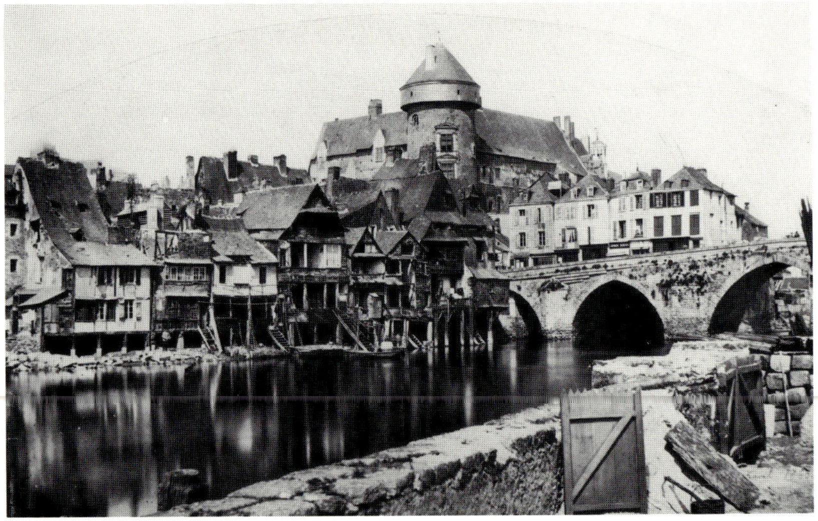

125. UNIDENTIFIED PHOTOGRAPHER
View of the Chateau at Laval from across the Mayenne River

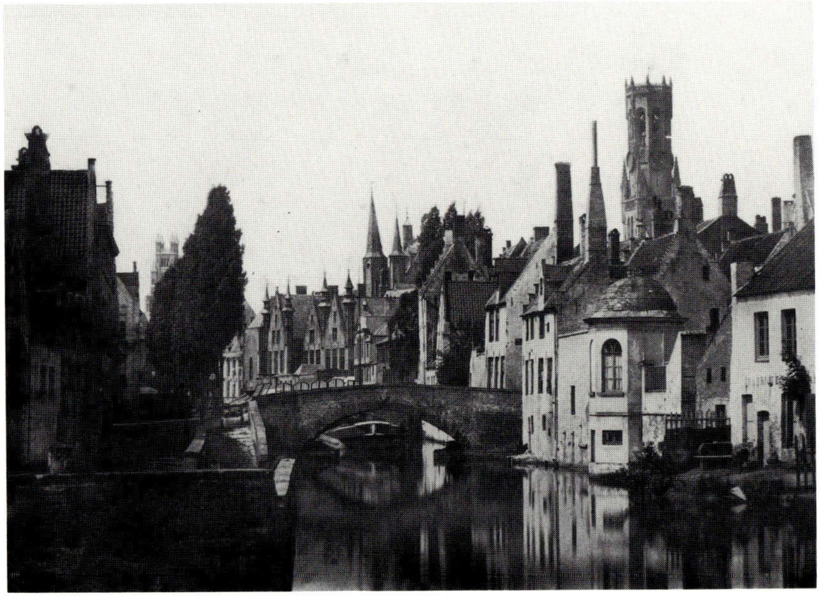

126. J. F. MICHIELS
Lateral View of the Franc de Bruges Taken from the Pont du Moulin

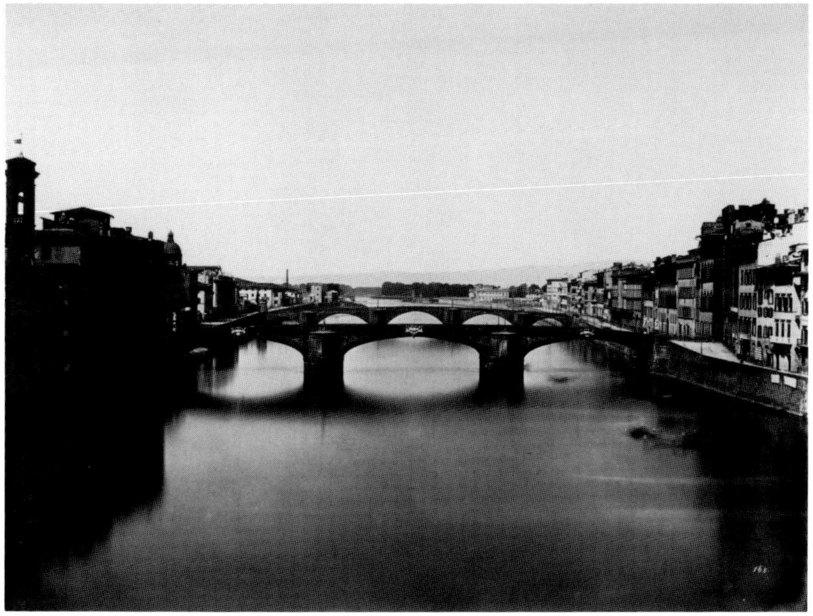

127. LEOPOLDO, ROMUALDO, and GIUSEPPE ALINARI
Florence: View of the Arno

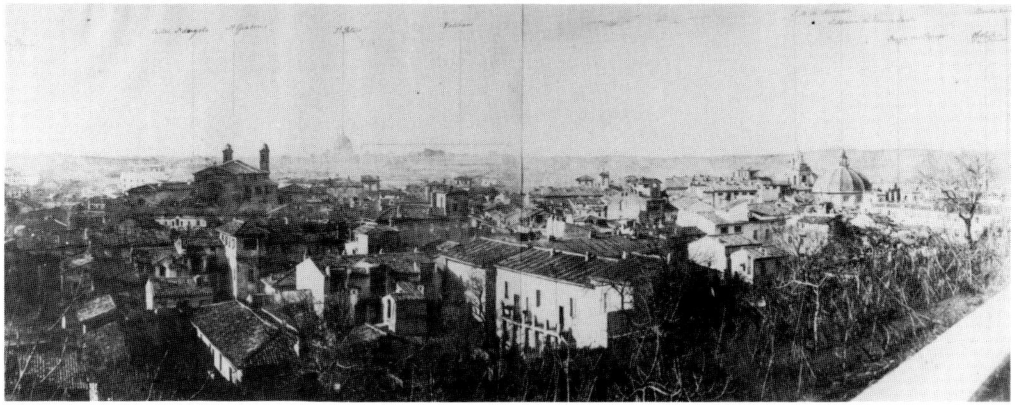

128. UNIDENTIFIED PHOTOGRAPHER
Panorama of Rome

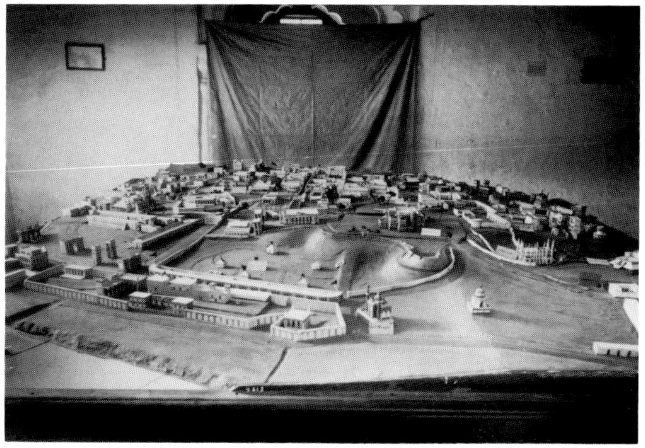

129. LALA DEEN DAYAL (RAJA)
Model of the Residency During the Siege of 1857—Lucknow

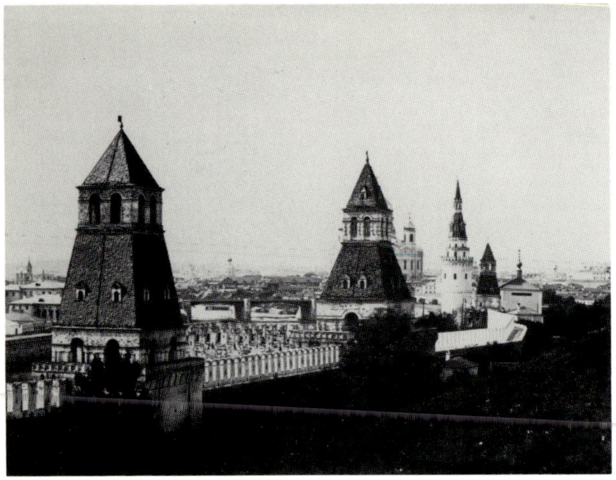

130. UNIDENTIFIED PHOTOGRAPHER
Moscow, View of the Kremlin

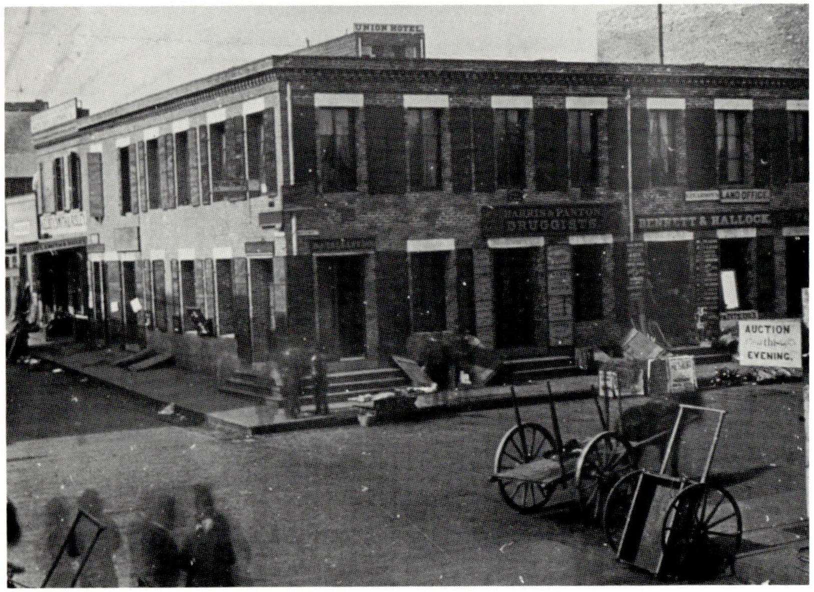

132. FREDERICK COOMBS
Montgomery Street, San Francisco

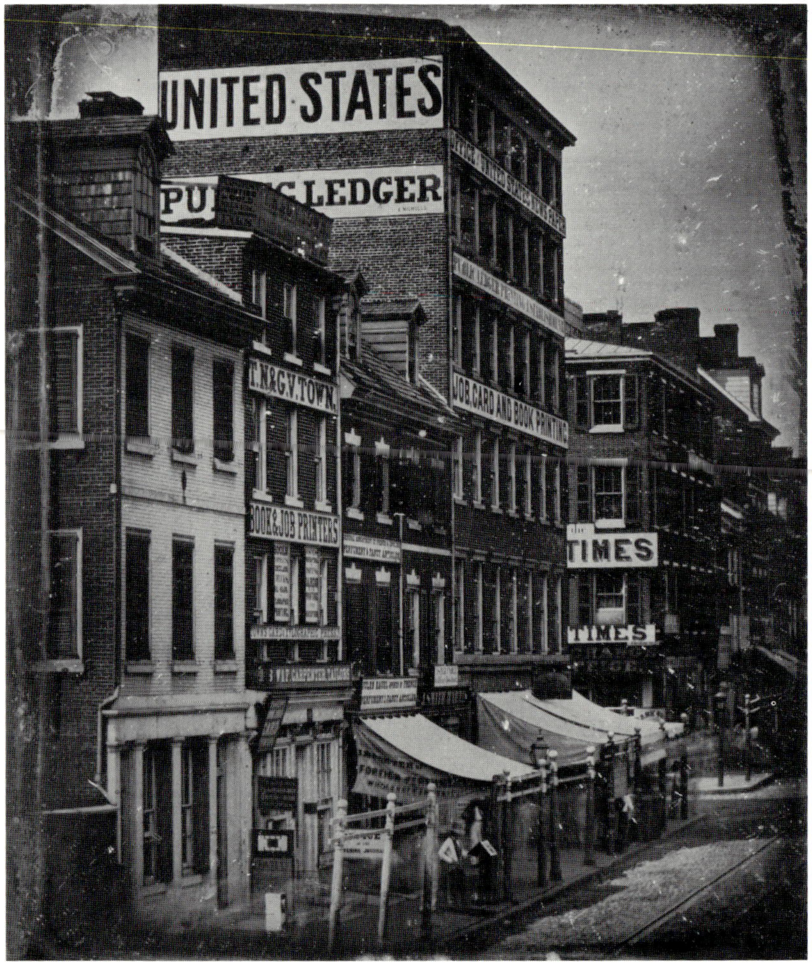

131. GEORGE READ
Philadelphia, 3rd and Chestnut Streets

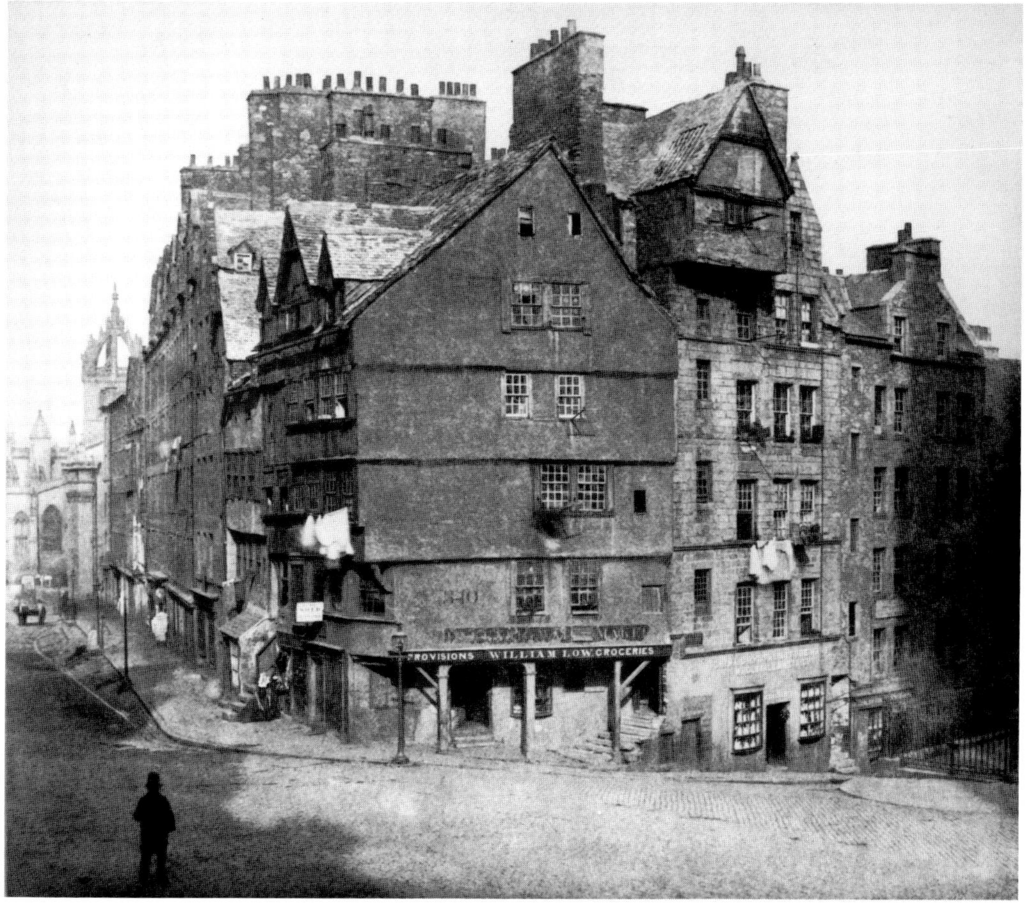

133. DR. THOMAS KEITH
The High Street, With John Knox's House, Edinburgh

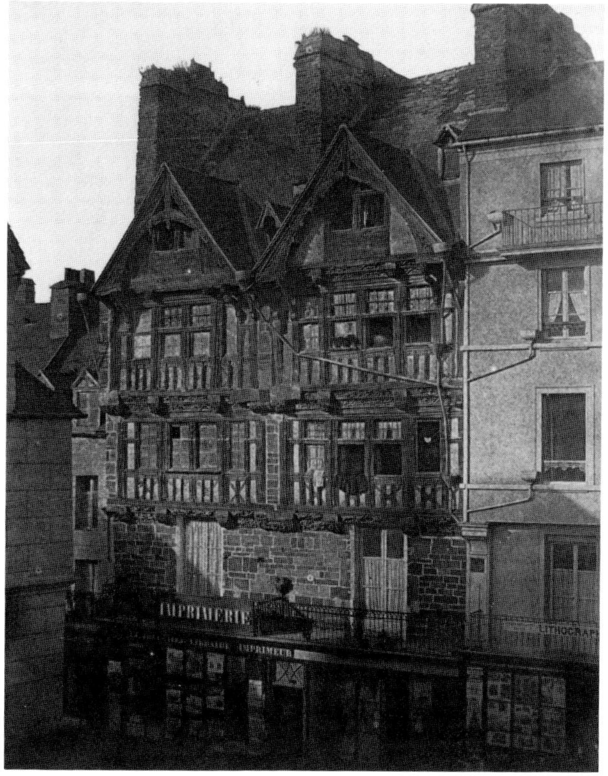

134. (LOUIS-DESIRE BLANQUART-EVRARD)
Frame House Occupied by Mr. Letriguilly's Bookstore, St. Lô

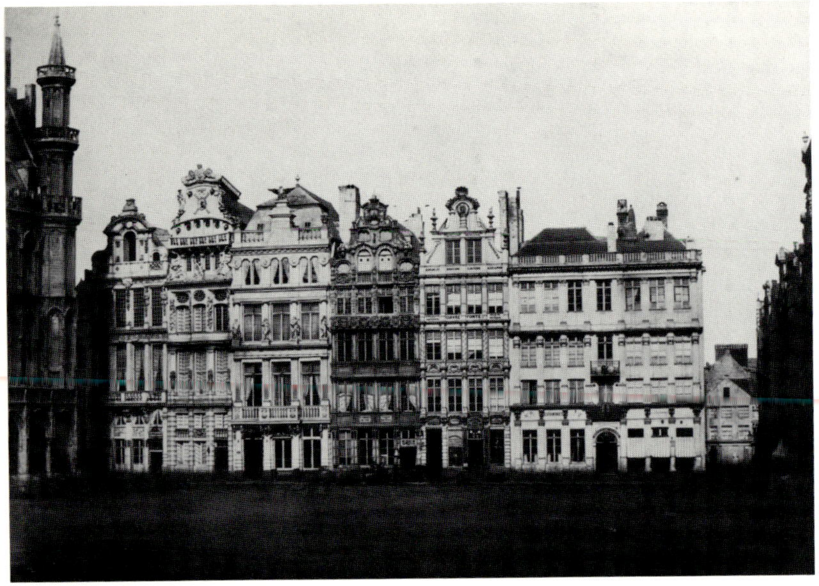

135. GUILLAUME CLAINE
Corporate Houses on the Grand Place, Brussels

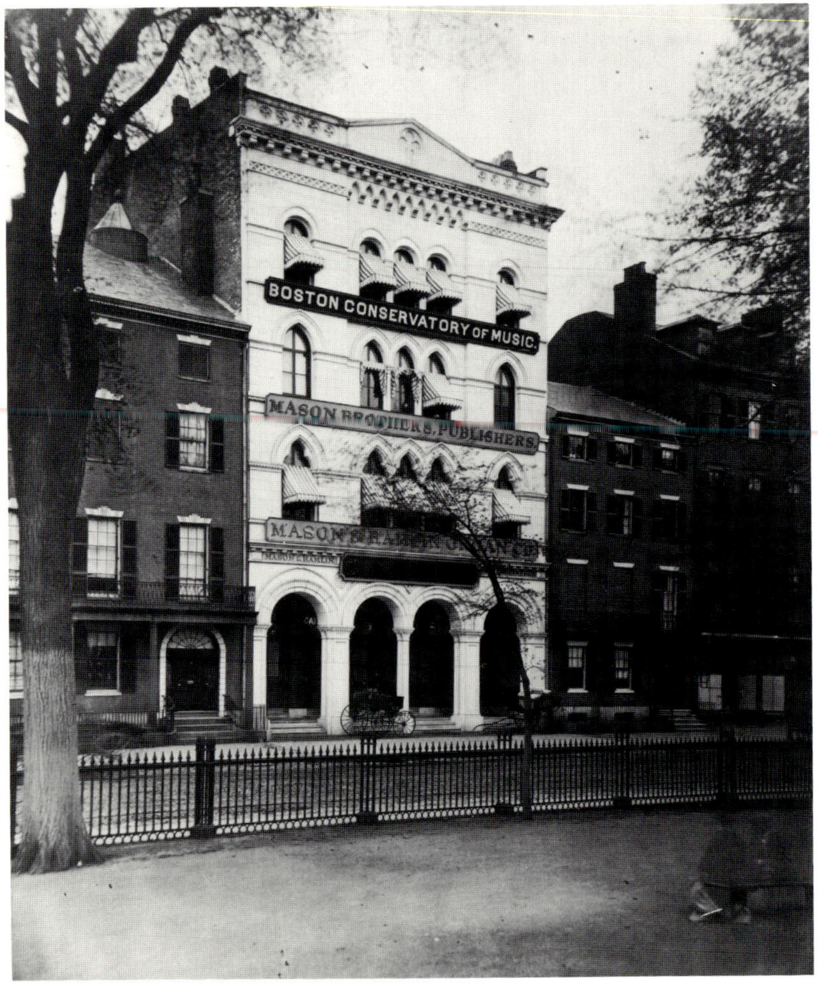

136. JOSIAH JOHNSON HAWES
Boston Conservatory of Music, Mason Brothers, Publishers, Mason & Hamlin Organ Co., Carriages

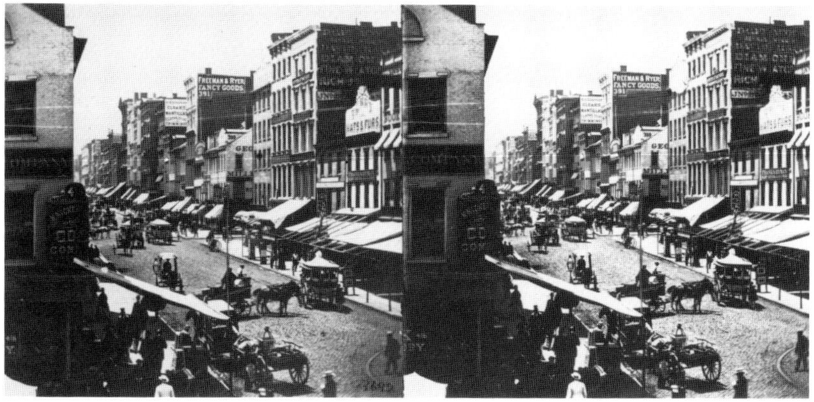

137. E. & H. T. ANTHONY
a. *Looking Up Broadway from the Corner of Canal Street*

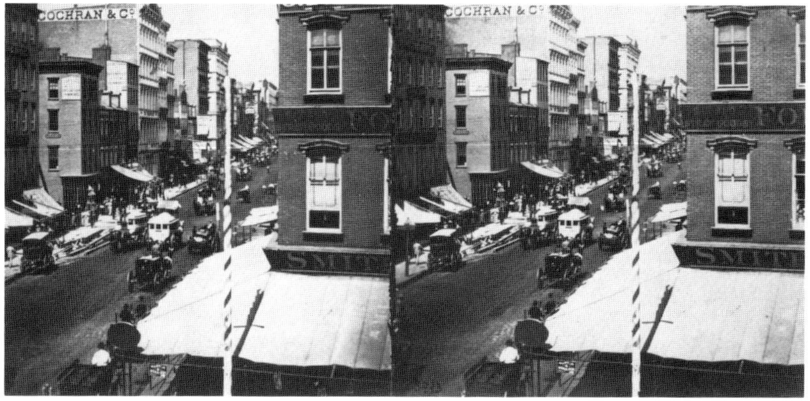

b. *Looking Down Broadway from the Corner of Canal Street*

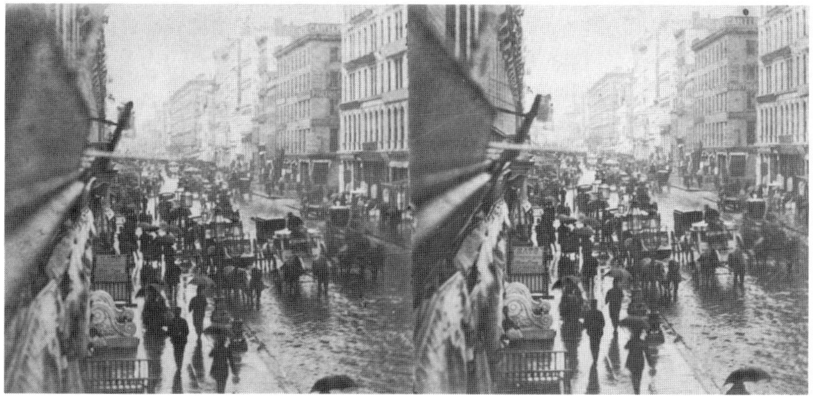

c. *Broadway on a Rainy Day*

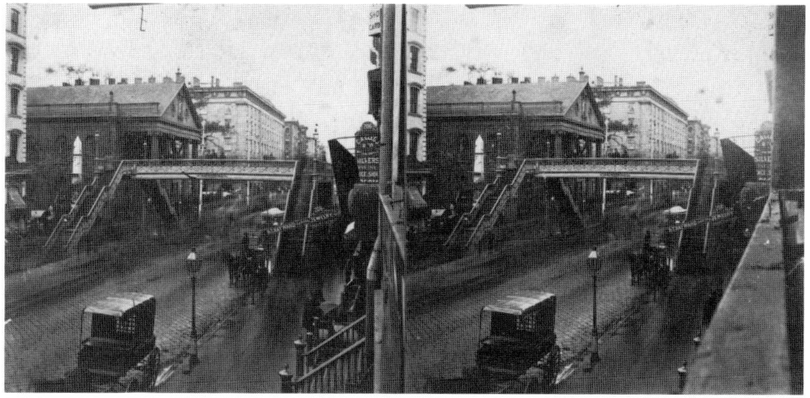

d. *The Broadway Bridge, Including St. Paul's Church and the Astor House*

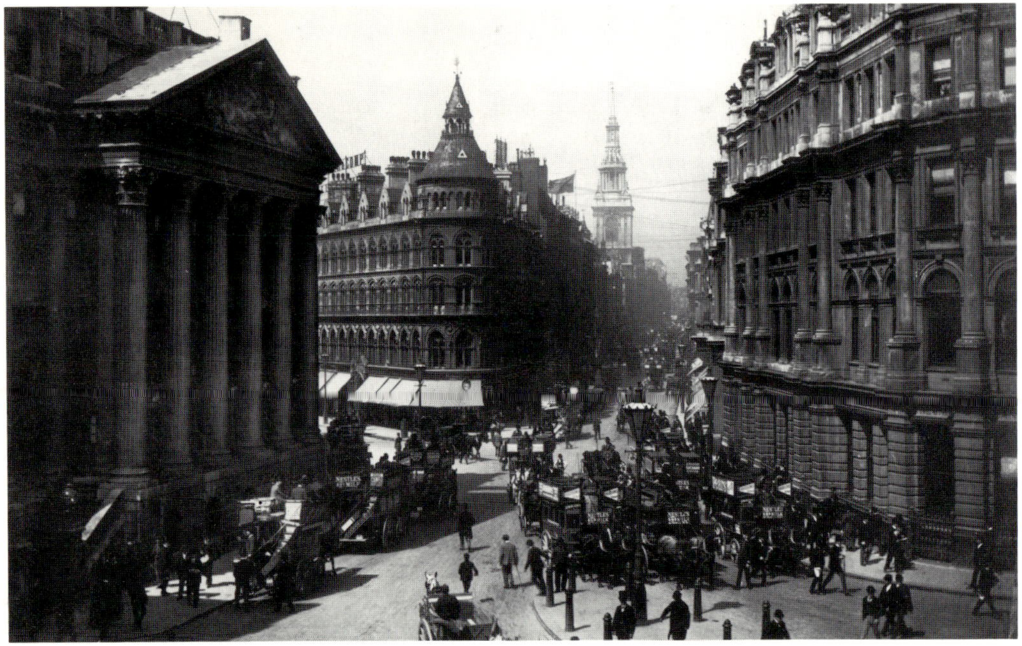

138. JAMES VALENTINE AND SONS
Cheapside, London

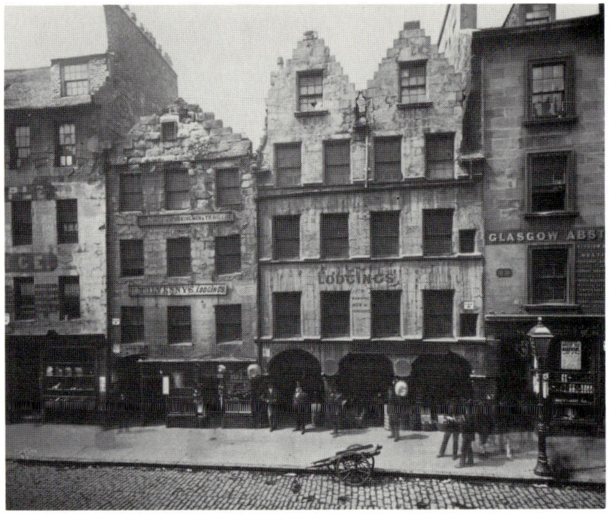

139. THOMAS ANNAN
Old Building, High Street

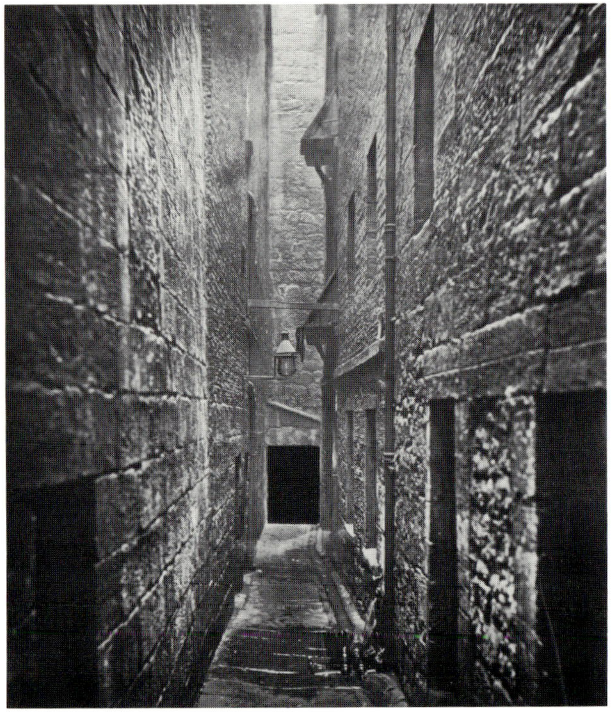

140. THOMAS ANNAN
Close No. 61, Saltmarket

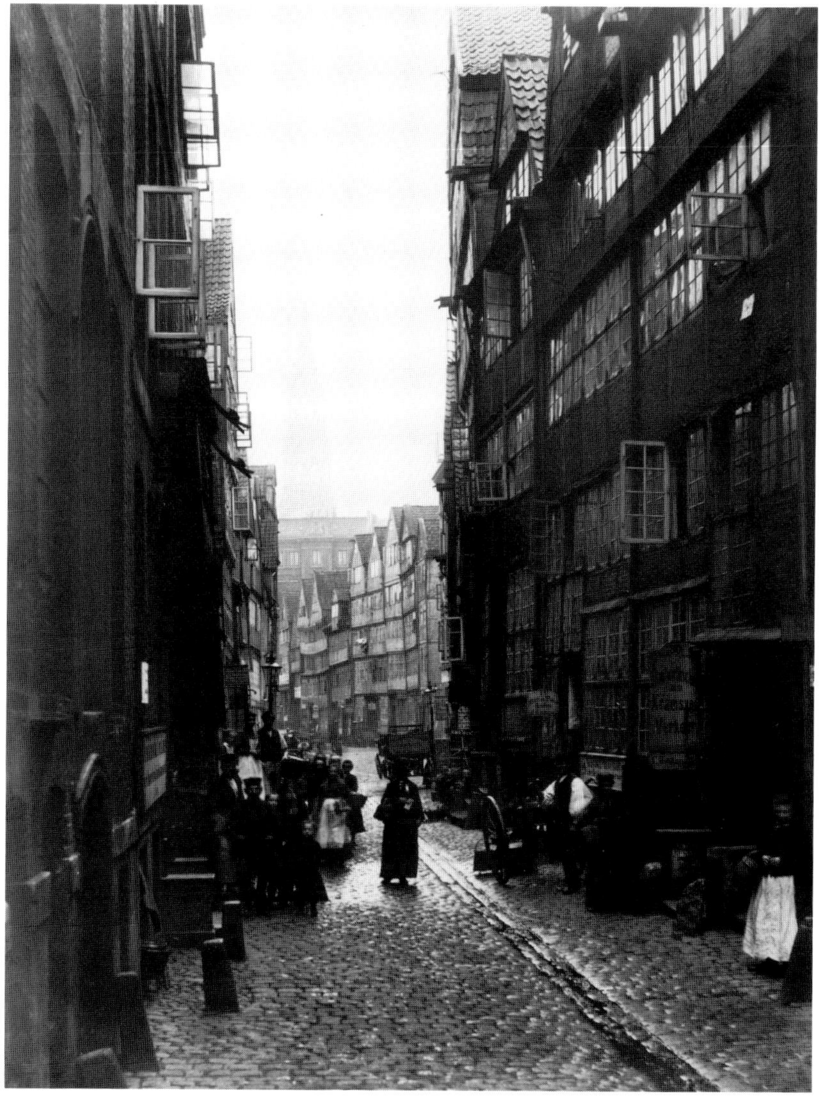

141. UNIDENTIFIED PHOTOGRAPHER
Dovenfleth from the Center End, Hamburg (Free Port)

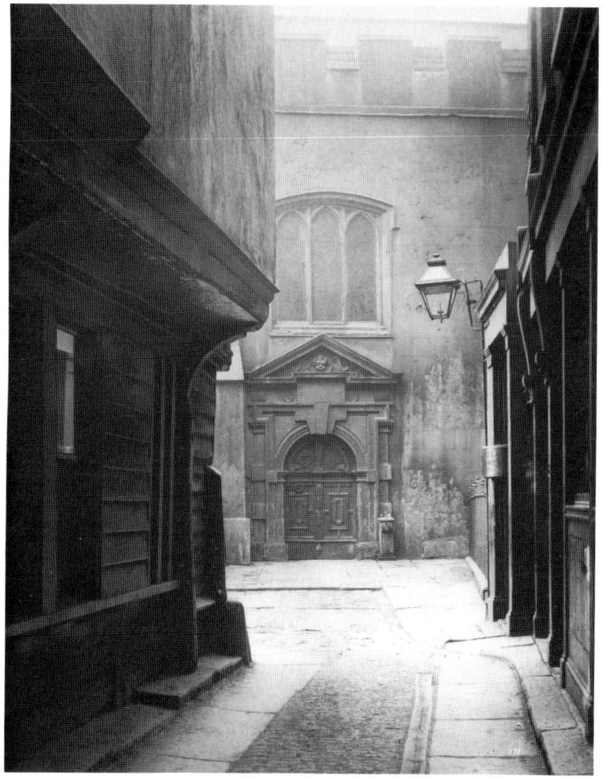

142. HENRY DIXON
Great Saint Helen's, London

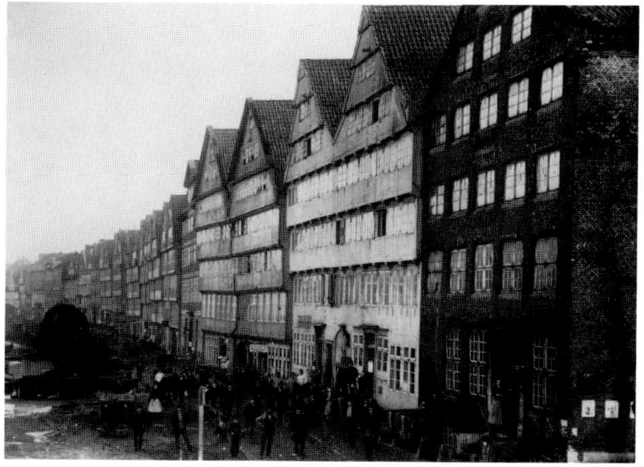

143. UNIDENTIFIED PHOTOGRAPHER
Dutch District, Hamburg (Free Port)

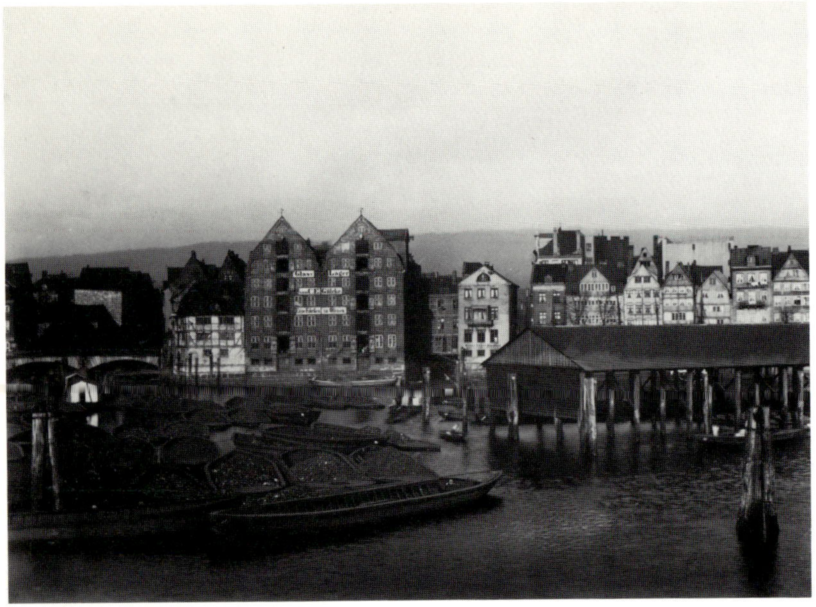

144. UNIDENTIFIED PHOTOGRAPHER
Hamburg, View from the Elbe

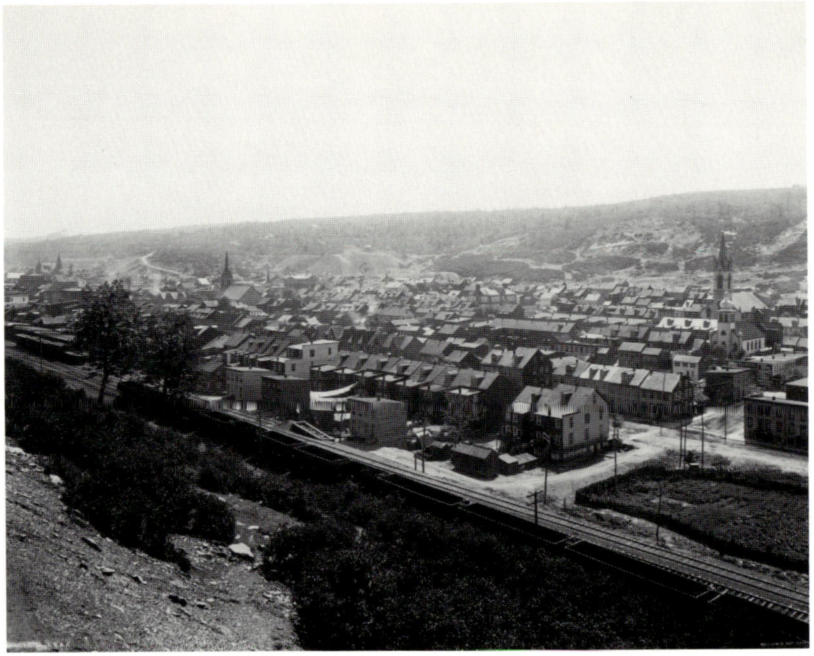

145. WILLIAM H. RAU
Mahanoy City, L.V.R.R.

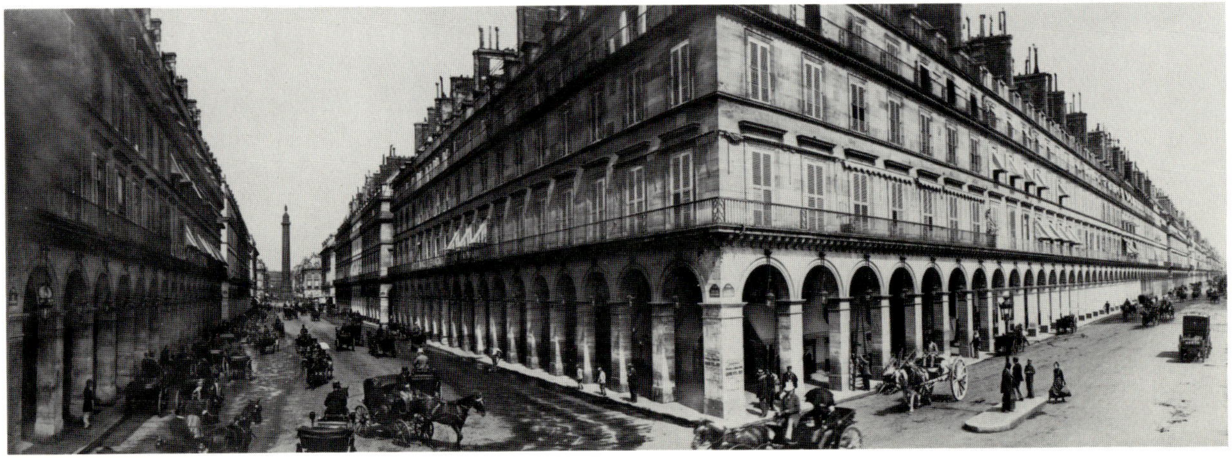

146. A. C. CHAMPAGNE
Perspective Along the rue de Castiglione, Panorama of Paris (120°). N. D. Phot. Moëssard Panoramic Camera. Perspective Along the rue de Rivoli.

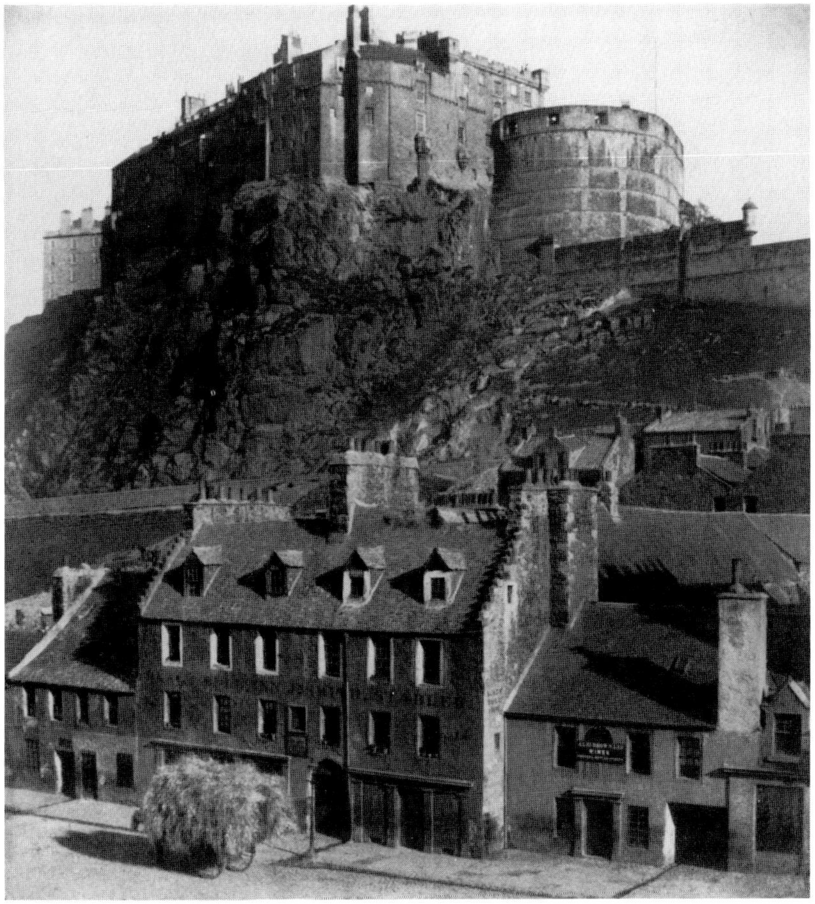

147. DR. THOMAS KEITH
Edinburgh Castle

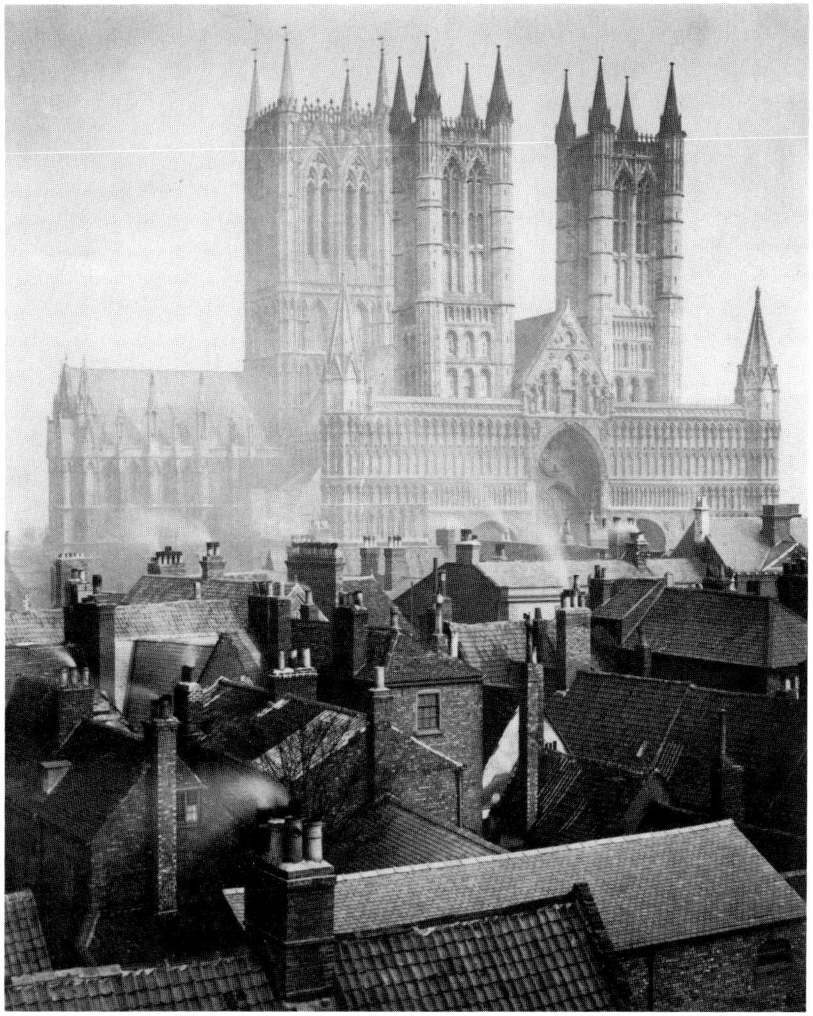

148. FREDERICK H. EVANS
Lincoln Cathedral from the Castle

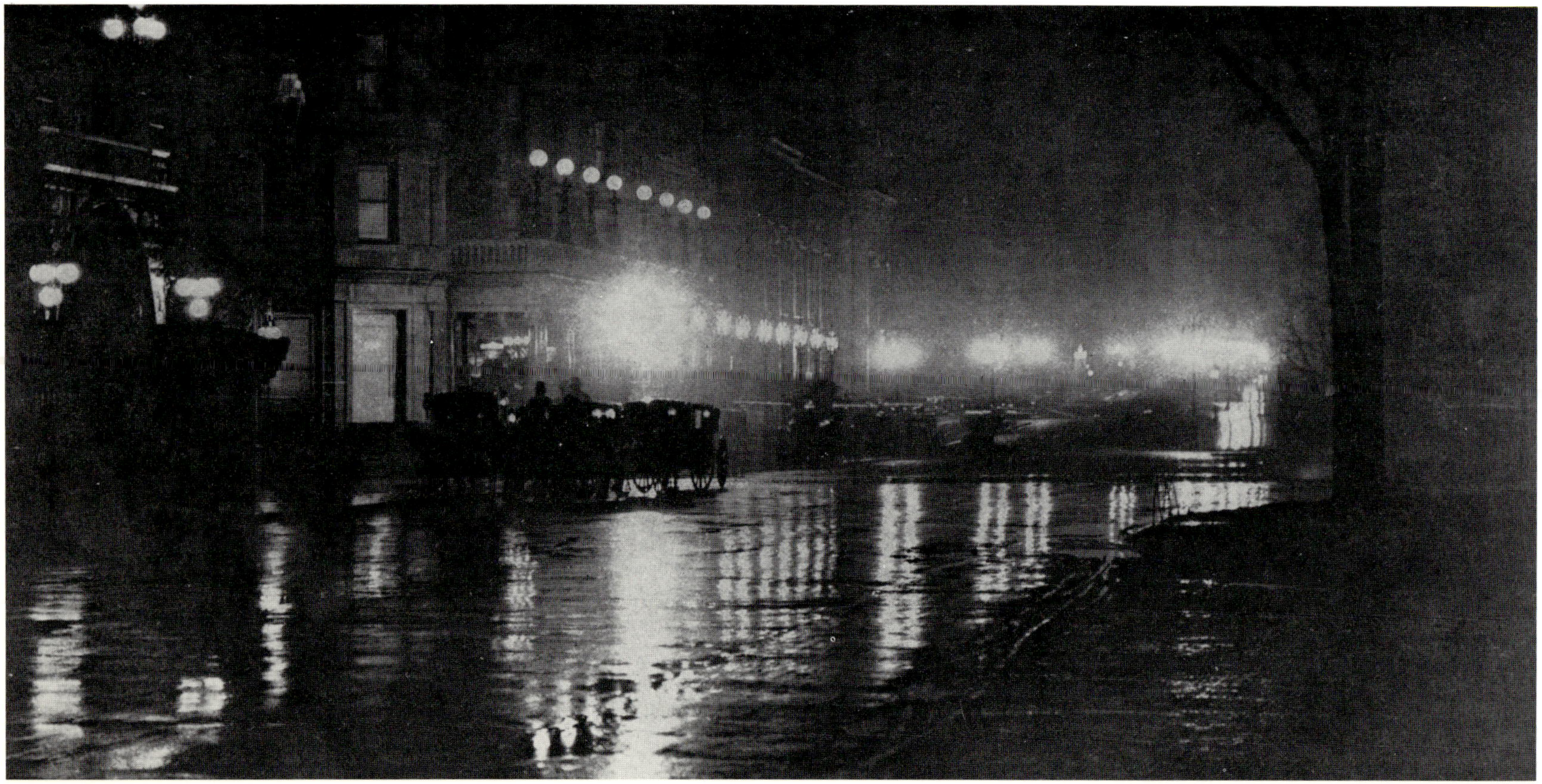

149. ALFRED STIEGLITZ
Reflections: Night—New York

CATALOGUE

The following catalogue is arranged by the six sections of the exhibition and follows the general layout of the exhibition at its premier at the George Eastman House. Within each section, the individual prints are chronologically listed by the general date of their subject matter, thereby allowing for how similar architecture was treated by differing photographers. Whenever a photographer's name is placed in parentheses, this indicates an attribution to that photographer. In a few instances, the photograph's date includes two different years separated by a "/"; the first year is the date of the negative, the second that of the exhibited print when that date is significantly different from the first. Wherever the source, whether it was an album, a portfolio of prints, or a publication, is known, this too has been included. Measurements are those of the image only; height preceding width. The final number in the entry is the Museum's accession number for that print.

I. ANTIQUITY AND ARCHAEOLOGY

1
(PIERRE GUSTAVE JOLY DE LOTBINIERE)
Canadian, b. Switzerland, 1798-France, 1865
Dakké and *Korti*
1840
Aquatints by Himely from daguerreotypes by Joly de Lotbinière
From: Hector Horeau, *Panorama d'Egypte et de Nubie*, Paris, 1841.
20.0 x 28.5 cm. and 19.8 x 28.9 on single sheet
Museum purchase
78:0701:1, 2

2
MAXIME DU CAMP
French, 1822-94
Nubia: Temple of Kardassy
ca. 1850
Salted paper print, printed by L.-D. Blanquart-Evrard
From: *Egypte, Nubie, Palestine et Syrie. Dessins photographiques recueillis pendant les années 1849, 1850 et 1851*, Paris, 1852.
16.5 x 21.8 cm.
Gift of Eastman Kodak Co., ex-collection Gabriel Cromer
79:0031:21

3
MAXIME DU CAMP
French, 1822-94
Nubia: Abu Simbel: Entrance of the Temple of Hathor
ca. 1850
Salted paper print, printed by L.-D. Blanquart-Evrard
From: *Egypte, Nubie, Palestine et Syrie. Dessins photographiques recueillis pendant les années 1849, 1850 et 1851*, Paris, 1852.
21.5 x 16.5 cm.
Gift of Eastman Kodak Co., ex-collection Gabriel Cromer
79:0031:42

4
ANTONIO BEATO
British, b. Italy, active 1855-ca. 70
Esne, Egypt: Temple of Khnum, Capitals of the Portico
ca. 1862-67
Albumen print
38.5 x 26.5 cm.
Museum purchase
76:0020:1

5
FRANCIS FRITH
British, 1822-98
The Great Pyramid, and the Great Sphinx
1858
Albumen print
From: *Egypt, Sinai and Jerusalem*, London, ca. 1858, pl. 17
39.1 x 49.2 cm.
Museum purchase
79:0068:17

6
FRANCIS FRITH
British, 1822-98
The Hypaethral Temple, Philae
1858
Albumen print
From: *Egypt, Sinai and Jerusalem*, London, ca. 1858, pl. 10
37.8 x 48.4 cm.
Museum purchase
79:0068:10

7
FRANK M. GOOD
British, active 1870s
Philae, Near View Hypaethral Temple
ca. 1870-75
Albumen print
16.2 x 21.1 cm.
Museum purchase
80:0316:1

8
AUGUST SALZMANN
French, 1824-72
Temple Courtyard, Jerusalem
1854
Salted paper print, printed by L.-D. Blanquart-Evrard
From: *Jerusalem, vues et monuments de la Ville Sainte de l'époque judaïque au present*, Paris, 1856.
23.3 x 33.6 cm.
Museum purchase
71:0117:9

9
JAMES ROBERTSON and FELICE BEATO
British team, active 1850s
The Tower of David, Jerusalem
ca. 1856-7
Albumen print
From: *Jerusalem*, Constantinople-Leipzig, 1864 (?)
33.0 x 25.1 cm.
Museum purchase, L.A.W. Fund
81:3227:6

10
FELIX BONFILS
French, 1831-85
Palmyra: Ruins of the Southern End of a Temple (Syria)
1877-78
Albumen print
From: *Souvenirs d'Orient. Album pittoresque des sites, villes et ruines les plus remarquables de la Terre Sainte*, Alais, 1878.
28.4 x 23.3 cm.
Museum purchase
73:0074:7

11
FELIX BONFILS
French, 1831-85
Baalbek: Portal of the Temple of Jupiter (Syria)
1877-78
Albumen print
From: *Souvenirs d'Orient. Album pittoresque des sites, villes et ruines les plus remarquables de la Terre Sainte*, Alais, 1878.
28.7 x 22.3 cm.
Museum purchase
86:0054:1

12
UNIDENTIFIED PHOTOGRAPHER
American
a. *Parthenon Colonnade, Athens*
b. *Devil at Entrance, Temple Mute*
c. *Lotus Columns, Temple Thothmes III, Karnak*
d. *Looking Up at Leaning Columns at Karnak*
1888
Gelatin silver prints (4)
Kodak no. 1 snapshots
Gifts of Mrs. Raymond K. Albright
74:0250:15, 74:0252:23, 74:0253:29, 74:0253:31

13
JAMES ROBERTSON and FELICE BEATO
British team, active 1850s
Imperial Door of the Old Seraglio—Constantinople
ca. 1885
Albumen print
31.5 x 25.8 cm.
Museum collection
81:3227:7

14
D. CONSTANTINE (or COSTANTIN)
Greek (?), active 1850s
The Acropolis at Athens, with the Temple of Jupiter
ca. 1859
Albumen print
26.9 x 37.3 cm.
Gift of Eastman Kodak Co., ex-collection Gabriel Cromer
80:0233:2

15
WILLIAM JAMES STILLMAN
American, 1828-1901
View of the Parthenon, Athens
1868-69
Carbon print
From: *The Acropolis of Athens, Illustrated Picturesquely and Architecturally in Photography*, London, 1870
18.7 x 24.1 cm. (domed top)
Gift of Robert J. Doherty
73:0127:8

16
(REVEREND CALVERT R. JONES)
British, ca. 1801-77
The Colosseum
1846
Salted paper print, printed by Nicolaas Henneman (?)
26.9 x 21.0 cm. (trimmed)
Gift of Alden Scott Boyer
81:2848:1

17
COUNT FREDERIC A. FLACHERON
French, 1813-83
The Roman Forum
1850
Salted paper print
33.8 x 24.9 cm.
Gift of Eastman Kodak Co., ex-collection Gabriel Cromer
82:1622:1

18
EDOUARD-DENIS BALDUS
French, b. Prussia, 1815-82
Amphitheater at Nimes
ca. 1854
Salted paper print
33.9 x 43.8 cm.
Gift of Eastman Kodak Co., ex-collection Gabriel Cromer
74:0050:18

19
ROBERT MACPHERSON
Scottish, 1811-72
Arch of Constantine—South Façade
ca. 1858
Albumen print
32.6 x 41.7 cm.
Museum purchase
76:0020:45

20
ROBERT MACPHERSON
Scottish, 1811-72
Temple of the Sibyl at Tivoli
ca. 1858
Albumen print
37.4 x 31.6 cm.
Museum purchase
76:0020:51

21
GIOACCHINO ALTOBELLI (and POMPEO MOLINS ?)
Italian team, active 1860s
Ruins of the Thermae of Caracalla
ca. 1865
Albumen print
26.8 x 38.0 cm.
Museum purchase
76:0020:5

22a
UNIDENTIFIED PHOTOGRAPHER
French (?)
Inside View of the Principal Entrance of the Jumma Musjid
ca. 1856
Calotype negative, with ink
52.8 x 41.6 cm.
Museum collection
86:0053:1

22b
UNIDENTIFIED PHOTOGRAPHER
French (?)
Inside View of the Principal Entrance of the Jumma Musjid
ca. 1856
Albumenized salted paper print
51.6 x 41.0 cm. (trimmed)
Museum collection
86:0052:1

23
LIEUTENANT SENIOR
British, active 1860s
The Taj Mahal, Agra
ca. 1865
Albumen print
16.7 x 23.1 cm.
Museum purchase
77:0689:51

24
UNIDENTIFIED PHOTOGRAPHER
British
Entry Portal, India
ca. 1860s
Albumen print
16.2 x 18.3 cm.
Museum purchase
77:0689:86

25
SAMUEL BOURNE
British, 1834-1912
Benares: Vishnu Pud and Other Temples Near the Burning Ghât
ca. 1863-66
Albumen print
From: "Indian Photographs, T.S.," Manchester, ca. 1866-67, folio 12r.
23.6 x 29.4 cm.
Gift of Eastman Kodak Co., ex-collection Gabriel Cromer
79:0004:11

26
CLAUDE-JOSEPH-DESIRE CHARNAY
French, 1828-1915
Nunnery, Uxmal, Mexico
ca. 1858-60
Albumen print
From: "Monuments Aztèques du Méxique," Paris, ca. 1861, pl. 27
28.0 x 40.4 cm.
Gift of Eastman Kodak Co., ex-collection Gabriel Cromer
73:0199:27

27
TIMOTHY O'SULLIVAN
American, 1840-82
Old Mission Church, Zuni Pueblo, N.M., View from the Plaza
1873
Albumen print
From: *Photographs Showing Landscapes, Geological and other Features, of Portions of the Western Territory of the United States, Obtained in Connection with Geographical and Geological Explorations and Surveys West of the 100th Meridian, 1st Lieut. Geo. M. Wheeler, Corps of Engineers, U.S. Army, In Charge*, Washington, D.C., 1874-75, pl. 18 (Survey of 1873)
20.0 x 27.4 cm.
Museum purchase
79:0014:58

28
UNIDENTIFIED PHOTOGRAPHER
Japanese (?)
Fushimi Inari, Kioto, Shinto
ca. 1890s
Albumen print, hand colored
21.1 x 27.2 cm.
Museum purchase
74:0034:24

II. EUROPEAN HISTORY

29
LOUIS-AUGUSTE and AUGUSTE-ROSALIE BISSON
French, L.-A.: 1814-76; A.-R.: 1826-1900
Notre-Dame of Paris
ca. 1859
Photogravure print (Riffaut process), printed by Mme. A. Riffaut
35.7 x 27.1 cm.
Museum collection
77:0033:14

30
GUSTAVE (?)
French, active 1850s, 1860s
Cathedral of Saint Julien, Le Mans, from Place des Jacobins
ca. 1862
Albumen print
33.6 x 45.6 cm.
Museum collection
70:0049:5

31
LOUIS-AUGUSTE and AUGUSTE-ROSALIE BISSON
French, L.-A.: 1814-76; A.-R.: 1826-1900
Saint Vulfran, Abbeville, Western Façade
ca. 1856
Albumen print
43.4 x 35.8 cm.
Museum collection
81:1009:4

32
HENRI DESTOURNELLES LE SECQ
French, 1818-82
Selestat: Eglise St. Georges
1851
Salted paper print
32.2 x 22.8 cm.
Museum purchase
81:1465:1

33
ALEXANDER WILSON
British, active 1870s
Lichfield Cathedral: The Center Pillar in the Chapter House
ca. 1870
Albumen print
Stereographic card
Museum purchase
81:8694:13

34
(LOUIS-DESIRE BLANQUART-EVRARD)
French, 1802-72
Turret Finial, St. Pierre, Caen
ca. 1855
Albumenized salted paper print
26.3 x 19.9 cm.
Gift of Kodak Pathé, Vincennes, via the Société française de photographie; ex-collection Henri Fontan
81:1110:17

35
DAVID OCTAVIUS HILL (and) ROBERT ADAMSON
Scottish, Hill: 1802-70; Adamson: 1821-48
Linlithgow Palace, Niches Over the Entrance
ca. 1845
Salted paper print
14.6 x 18.6 cm.
Gift of Alden Scott Boyer
81:2396:45

36
CHARLES MARVILLE
French, 1816-79
The Red Door. Northern Doorway of Notre-Dame, Paris
1851
Salted paper print
20.7 x 15.5 cm.
Museum collection
81:1117:1

37
CHARLES CHENEY
British, active 1850s
Tilleshall Abbey
ca. 1857
Albumen print
17.7 x 22.3 cm.
Museum purchase
82:2615:3

38
GENEVIEVE-ELISABETH DISDERI
French, ca. 1817-78
Interior of St. Mathieu
ca. 1856
Albumen print
From: *Brest et ses environs*, Brest, ca. 1856, pl. 6
26.8 x 20.0 cm.
Museum collection
80:0256:18

39
GABRIEL BLAASE
French, active 1870s
Portal of the Maison Tristan
ca. 1875
Albumen print
24.3 x 17.0 cm.
Gift of Eastman Kodak Co., ex-collection Gabriel Cromer
82:1653:1

40
LOUIS-AUGUSTE and AUGUSTE-ROSALIE BISSON
French, L.-A.: 1814-76; A.-R.: 1826-1900
Guildhall, Yprès
ca. 1855
Albumen print
32.5 x 41.1 cm.
Gift of Eastman Kodak Co., ex-collection Gabriel Cromer
85:0514:1

41
R. MURRAY
British, active 1860s
Carnarvon Castle
1868
Albumen print
18.9 x 23.8 cm.
Museum purchase
77:0689:150

42
FRANCIS BEDFORD
British, 1816-94
Carnarvon Castle, Interior, from the Eagle Tower
ca. 1871
Albumen print
Stereographic card
Museum collection
81:6434:13

43
GEORGE WASHINGTON WILSON
Scottish, 1823-93
Windsor Castle, The Garden Terrace
ca. 1878
Albumen print
Stereographic card
Museum purchase
81:8700:153

44
FRANTISEK JOSEF FRIDRICH
Czechoslovakian, 1829-1892
Prague: Tower Bridge, Old City
ca. 1865
Albumen print
From: *Praha Staroměstská mostecká věž*, Prague, ca. 1865
25.7 x 20.7 cm.
Gift of Eastman Kodak Co., ex-collection Gabriel Cromer
80:0306:1

45
(CARLO PONTI)
Italian, ca. 1828-1900
Detail of the Ducal Palace, Venice
ca. 1862
Albumen print
32.4 x 26.5 cm.
Museum purchase
76:0020:78

46
CHARLES CLIFFORD
British, died 1863
Patio of the Léones y Fuente, The Alhambra
ca. 1856
Albumen print
31.0 x 43.7 cm.
Museum purchase
72:0122:2

47
(FR. ALPH. FORTIER)
French, died 1882
François I Wing and Staircase, Chateau de Blois
ca. 1856
Salted paper print
From: *Revue générale de l'architecture et des travaux publics*, 1856, pl. 21
24.6 x 18.8 cm.
Museum purchase, Horace W. Goldsmith Fund
85:1405:1

48
(LOUIS-DESIRE BLANQUART-EVRARD)
French, 1802-72
François I Wing and Staircase, Chateau de Blois
ca. 1855
Salted paper print
From: *Cahier 3*
20.4 x 25.4 cm.
Gift of Kodak Pathé, Vincennes, via the Société française de photographie; ex-collection Henri Fontan
81:1114:6

49
WILLIAM HENRY FOX TALBOT
British, 1800-77
Oxford
ca. 1843
Salted paper print
16.4 x 21.0 cm.
Gift of Miss M. I. Talbot
81:2847:8

50
UNIDENTIFIED PHOTOGRAPHER
German
Holstentor, Lübeck
ca. 1890
Collotype print
27.3 x 23.4 cm.
Museum collection
74:0109:5

51
LADISLAS CHODZKIEWICZ
Polish, active 1850s
Courtyard of Farewells, Palais de Fontainebleau
1853
Salted paper print
19.6 x 43.2 cm.
Gift of Eastman Kodak Co., ex-collection Gabriel Cromer
81:2932:1

52
(CARLO PONTI)
Italian, ca. 1828-1900
View of the Piazza di San Marco
ca. 1870
Albumen print
26.0 x 32.4 cm.
Museum purchase
82:2007:10

53
(FR. ALPH. FORTIER)
French, died 1882
Interior of the Louvre Courtyard
1853
Salted paper print
19.5 x 24.9 cm.
Gift of Alden Scott Boyer
81:1107:2

54
(REVEREND CALVERT R. JONES)
British, ca. 1804-77
View of the Piazza Navona, Rome
ca. 1846
Salted paper print, printed by Nicolaas Henneman (?)
21.0 x 26.9 cm.
Museum collection
81:2848:10

55
JAMES ANDERSON
British, 1813-77
Santa Maria in Aracoeli, Rome
ca. 1858
Albumen print
19.1 x 25.6 cm.
Museum purchase
76:0336:36

56
LOUIS-AUGUSTE and AUGUSTE-ROSALIE BISSON
French, L.-A.: 1814-76; A.-R.: 1826-1900
Tournament Court, Castle of Heidelberg
ca. 1859
Albumen print
43.4 x 34.0 cm. (domed top)
Museum collection
81:1011:1

57
LEOPOLDO, ROMUALDO, and GIUSEPPE ALINARI
Italian, L.: 1832-65; R.: 1830-91; G.: 1836-91
Florence: The Piazzale degli Uffizi
ca. 1854-65
Albumen print
34.3 x 25.0 cm.
Museum purchase
76:0020:23

58
FERDINANDO ONGANIA
Italian, 1842-1911
Courtyard of the Ducal Palace and the Giants' Staircase
ca. 1891-92
Photogravure print
From: *Calli e Canali in Venezia*, Venice, 1900, pl. 33
37.5 x 22.6 cm.
Museum purchase
78:0052:33

59
UNIDENTIFIED PHOTOGRAPHER
French
The Place de la Concorde, Paris
ca. 1842
Daguerreotype
Quarter plate
Gift of Eastman Kodak Co., ex-collection Gabriel Cromer
76:0168:14

III. CONTEMPORARY ARCHITECTURAL EXPRESSIONS

60
DAVID OCTAVIUS HILL and ROBERT ADAMSON
Scottish, Hill: 1802-70; Adamson: 1821-48
Sir Walter Scott Monument, Edinburgh, Under Construction
ca. 1844
Salted paper print
19.8 x 15.0 cm.
Gift of Alden Scott Boyer
81:2398:35

61
JOHN SHAW SMITH
Irish, 1811-73
Modern Church in Athens
ca. 1851-52
Salted paper print
16.8 x 22.1 cm.
Gift of Alden Scott Boyer
81:1683:334

62
UNIDENTIFIED PHOTOGRAPHER
French
Church with "Doric" Façade
ca. 1844
Daguerreotype
Half plate
Gift of Eastman Kodak Co., ex-collection Gabriel Cromer
69:0265:121

63
DAVID OCTAVIUS HILL and ROBERT ADAMSON
Scottish, Hill: 1802-70; Adamson: 1821-48
The Royal Institution with the Castle in the Background
ca. 1844
Salted paper print
21.4 x 16.3 cm. (untrimmed)
Gift of Alden Scott Boyer
81:2398:34

64
HUARD
French, active Russia, 1860s
Arch of Triumph, St. Petersburg, 1838
1862
Albumen print
16.1 x 22.5 cm. (rounded corners)
Gift of Eastman Kodak Co., ex-collection Gabriel Cromer
80:0372:3

65
UNIDENTIFIED PHOTOGRAPHER
American
A Rural Residence
ca. 1845
Daguerreotype
Sixth plate
Gift of the Wisconsin Historical Society
79:3190:4

66
LEON TRIPIER
French, active 1850s
The Author's House
Salted paper print
30.8 x 24.9 cm.
Museum collection
82:1641:4

67
UNIDENTIFIED PHOTOGRAPHER
American
Monumental Church, Richmond, Virginia
ca. 1849
Daguerreotype
Quarter plate
Museum collection
82:1565:1

68
UNIDENTIFIED PHOTOGRAPHER
French
Guard House, Place Bellecour, Lyons
ca. 1854
Salted paper print
22.3 x 32.0 cm.
Museum collection
82:1641:1

69
UNIDENTIFIED PHOTOGRAPHER
American
United States Treasury Building
ca. 1870
Albumen print
19.5 x 25.1 cm. (trimmed)
Gift of 3M Company, ex-collection Louis Walton Sipley
77:0296:7

70
UNIDENTIFIED PHOTOGRAPHER
American
New York Stock Exchange
ca. 1905
Gelatin silver print
39.4 x 31.0 cm.
Museum collection
68:0329:54

71
EDOUARD-DENIS BALDUS
French, b. Prussia, 1815-82
The New Louvre: Pavillon d'Horloge
ca. 1856-57
Albumen print
43.6 x 33.4 cm.
Gift of Eastman Kodak Co., ex-collection Gabriel Cromer
74:0050:12

72
EDOUARD-DENIS BALDUS
French, b. Prussia, 1815-82
The New Louvre: Pavillon Richelieu (Detail)
ca. 1856-57
Albumen print
33.3 x 43.4 cm.
Gift of Eastman Kodak Co., ex-collection Gabriel Cromer
74:0050:7

73
CHARLES NEGRE
French, 1820-80
Imperial Asylum at Vincennes
1858-59
Albumen print
42.3 x 32.8 cm.
Museum purchase
85:1405:3

74
UNIDENTIFIED PHOTOGRAPHER
German or French
The Zwinger, Interior Courtyard, Dresden
ca. 1870
Albumen print
23.2 x 47.9 cm.
Gift of Dr. Walter Clark
81:3245:1

75
ISAIAH WEST TABER
American, 1830-1912
Grand and Palace Hotels, San Francisco, Cal.
ca. 1885
Albumen print
18.8 x 24.2 cm.
Gift of Alden Scott Boyer
81:2265:33

76
(JOSIAH JOHNSON HAWES)
American, 1808-1901
Octagonal Building, Boston (?)
ca. 1855
Salted paper print
17.1 cm. (diam.)
Gift of 3M Company, ex-collection Louis Walton Sipley
77:0670:3

77
VICTOR PREVOST
French, 1820-81
Bridge No. 3, September 23
1862
Albumen print
From: *Central Park*, New York, 1862, pl. 11
13.9 x 13.1 cm.
Museum purchase
76:0031:11

78
FREDERICK GUTEKUNST
American, 1831-1917
Sanctuary & Grand Altar of the Cathedral of St. Peter & St. Paul, Philadelphia
1865
Albumen print
33.4 x 25.6 cm.
Museum collection
70:0049:43

79
(HYACINTHE CESAR or CLEMENCE JACOB DELMAET and LOUIS-EMILE DURANDELLE)
French team, active 1860s-80s
Stairwell Interior in Ruins
ca. 1871
Albumen print
43.1 x 28.5 cm.
Museum collection
86:0048:1

80
UNIDENTIFIED PHOTOGRAPHER
German
Kitchen of the Home Economics School for Poor Young Women in Kiel
ca. 1875
Albumen print
23.5 x 28.7 cm.
Museum collection
86:0045:1

81
LOUIS-ALPHONSE DAVANNE
French, 1824-1912
The Governor's Salon, Algiers, Mirror Effect
ca. 1875
Albumen print
29.6 x 23.3 cm.
Museum collection
83:1339:3

82
(LOUIS-DESIRE BLANQUART-EVRARD)
French, 1802-72
Triumphal Arch, Belgium, to Commemorate the Reign of Leopold I
1856
Albumenized salted paper print
From: *Cahier 3*
23.2 x 18.3 cm.
Gift of Kodak Pathé, Vincennes, via the Société française de photographie; ex-collection Henri Fontan
81:1114:13

83
UNIDENTIFIED PHOTOGRAPHER
American
Machinery Hall, View from the Southwest Corner of the Manufacturers and Liberal Arts Building
1893
Photogravure (photomezzotint) print, printed by Goupil, Paris
From: D. Appleton & Co., *The Art of the World, Illustrated in the Paintings, Statuary, and Architecture of the World's Columbian Exposition*, New York, 1893, part XIX.
21.5 x 29.4 cm.
Gift of 3M Company, ex-collection Louis Walton Sipley
77:0578:1

84
JEAN-EUGENE-AUGUSTE ATGET
French, 1857-1927
Art Nouveau Store, 45 rue St. Augustin, Paris
ca. 1904-5
Albumen print
17.7 x 22.0 cm. (irregular)
Museum purchase
78:1628:27

85
ALBERT LEVY
French, active ca. 1900
Apartment Building, Corner of Rue de Mogador and Rue Joubert, Paris, 9th Arrondisement
ca. 1905
Cyanotype print
30.0 x 24.9 cm. (irregular)
Museum purchase
86:0085:1

IV. THE RUSTIC AND THE VERNACULAR

86
VICTOR PREVOST
French, 1820-81
Corner of a Farm
ca. 1855
Salted paper print
24.5 x 32.6 cm.
Gift of William Fletcher
74:0021:2

87
(CHARLES MARVILLE)
French, 1816-79
Lamb Shed at the Jardin des Plantes, Paris
1851
Salted paper print
From: L.-D. Blanquart-Evrard, *Mélanges photographiques*, Lille, 1851.
15.6 x 20.7 cm.
Gift of Alden Scott Boyer
81:1108:6

88
JOHN PERCY and JOHN SPILLER
British team, active 1856
The New Mill, Near Lynton, North Devon
1856
Albumen print
From: *Photographic Album for the Year 1857*, London, 1857, pl. 28.
30.0 x 23.4 cm.
Museum collection
79:1992:28

89
PETER HENRY EMERSON
British, 1856-1936
Farm Scene, Woman Carrying Bucket
ca. 1888
Platinum print
28.6 x 20.2 cm.
Museum collection
81:1285:30

90
GEORGE N. BARNARD
American, 1819-1902
The John Ross House, Ringold, Georgia
1864
Albumen print
From: *Photographic Views of Sherman's Campaign, . . . From negatives taken in the field by Geo. N. Barnard, Official Photographer of the Military Div. of the Miss.*, New York, 1866, pl. 16.
25.5 x 35.8 cm.
Museum purchase
81:0001:16

91
FELICE BEATO
British, b. Italy, active 1855-ca. 67
Exterior of Fort Taku, Northern China, Showing French Entrance
1860
Albumen print
22.5 x 29.3 cm.
Museum purchase
76:0134:3

92
TIMOTHY O'SULLIVAN
American, 1840-82
Signal Tower on Elk Mountain, Maryland, Overlooking Battlefield of Antietam
1862/65
Albumen print
From: Alexander Gardner, *Gardner's Photographic Sketchbook of the War*, Washington, D.C., 1865, pl. 22
22.5 x 17.7 cm.
Museum collection
81:2858:22

93
TIMOTHY O'SULLIVAN
American, 1840-82
Camp Ruby, Ruby Valley, Nevada
1868
Albumen print
From: Clarence King, *Photographs: Geological Explorations of the 40th Parallel, Clarence King, Geologist in Charge*, Washington, D.C., various editions, 1867-76, no. 45.
21.0 x 28.0 cm.
Gift of Harvard University
81:1887:10

94
JOHN HYDE
British, active 1860s
A Porch in Chiefden Woods
1868
Albumen print
14.2 x 19.2 cm.
Museum purchase
77:0689:158

95
UNIDENTIFIED PHOTOGRAPHER
American
House and Boat House, View from the Dock
ca. 1890
Albumen print
From: Portfolio of the works of Frederick B. White, architect.
14.0 x 21.2 cm.
Museum collection
71:0128:5

96
FREDERICK DEBOURG RICHARDS
American, 1822-1903
John McAllister's House
1860
Salted paper print
18.4 x 13.4 cm. (rounded corners)
Gift of 3M Company, ex-collection Louis Walton Sipley
77:0392:28

97
UNIDENTIFIED PHOTOGRAPHER
British
Rural Cottage, Half-Timbered Construction
ca. 1865
Albumen print
16.2 x 20.4 cm.
Museum purchase
77:0689:67

98
UNIDENTIFIED PHOTOGRAPHER
American
Residence of Mr. C. S. French, Newport, Rhode Island
ca. 1890
Collotype print
23.0 x 28.0 cm.
Museum collection
74:0110:15

99
UNIDENTIFIED PHOTOGRAPHER
American
Mrs. Deecke's Kindergarten and Graded School
ca. 1895
Gelatin silver print
15.5 x 18.8 cm.
Museum collection
84:0023:1

100
FREDERICK H. EVANS
British, 1853-1943
Kelmscott Manor, Attics
ca. 1897
Platinum print
15.5 x 20.0 cm.
Museum purchase
81:1198:5

101
UNIDENTIFIED PHOTOGRAPHER
American
Mr. E. F. Hutton's "Camp Hutridge," The Indian Room
ca. 1905
Gelatin silver print
18.8 x 23.9 cm.
Museum collection
68:0329:5

102
ISAIAH WEST TABER
American, 1830-1912
Barnard's Hotel, Yosemite Valley, California
ca. 1885
Albumen print
12.4 x 19.3 cm.
Gift of Alden Scott Boyer
81:2265:19

103
JEAN-EUGENE-AUGUSTE ATGET
French, 1857-1927
Bagneux: Old Quarry Wells
1901
Albumen print
17.6 x 21.6 cm. (irregular)
Museum purchase
78:1628:33

V. CONSTRUCTION AND PROGRESS

104
UNIDENTIFIED PHOTOGRAPHER
French
Halles Centrales, Paris. View of the South-western Pavilion During Construction
1856
Photolithographic print (Poitevin process), printed by Alphonse Poitevin
From: *Revue générale de l'architecture et des travaux publics*, 1856, pl. 41.
16.6 x 23.5 cm. (oval)
Gift of Eastman Kodak Co., ex-collection Gabriel Cromer
85:0626:1

105
PHILIP HENRY DELAMOTTE
British, 1820-89
View in Central Hall, Art Treasures Exhibition, Manchester
1857
Albumen print
From: *Photographic Album for the Year 1857*, London, 1857, pl. 12.
22.8 x 17.7 cm.
Museum purchase
79:1992:12

106
J. A. WARWICK
British, active 1860s
The Conservatory
ca. 1865
Albumen print
From: *Chatsworth Photographs*, n.p., ca. 1865
12.1 x 17.3 cm.
Museum purchase
77:0854:30

107
ISAIAH WEST TABER
American, 1830-1912
Mr. D. O. Mills' Residence at Millbrae, Cal., View Near the Conservatory
ca. 1885
Albumen print
18.3 x 24.2 cm.
Gift of Alden Scott Boyer
81:2265:2

108
JOSEPH CUNDALL
British, 1818-95
The "Leviathan" During Its Construction. Sept. 21, 1855
1855
Albumen print
From: *The Leviathan*, London, 1858
22.8 x 28.7 cm.
Museum purchase
81:1647:21

109
CLARENCE LEANDER WEED
American, 1824-1903
Pacific Coast Scenery: Bridge at the Second Crossing of the Truckee River, Nevada, Central Pacific RR
ca. 1885
Albumen print, published by Thomas Houseworth
Carte-de-visite
Museum purchase
81:3822:68

110
ALBERT SANDS SOUTHWORTH and JOSIAH JOHNSON HAWES
American team, A. S.: 1811-94; J. J. H.: 1801-1901
J. A. Roebling's Suspension Bridge over the Niagara Gorge
ca. 1856
Daguerreotype
Whole plate
Museum purchase
74:0193:257a

111
WILLIAM HENRY JACKSON
American, 1843-1942
The Cantilever Bridge over Niagara River. M.C.R.R.
ca. 1900
Albumen print
43.8 x 95.5 cm.
Gift of Harvard University
81:2248:131

112
A. COLLARD
French, before 1840-after 1887
Roundhouse for 32 Locomotives at Nevers. First Interior View
1860-63
Albumen print
From: *Chemin de fer du Bourbonnais*, n.p., ca. 1860-63, pl. 28.
30.7 x 22.0 cm.
Gift of Eastman Kodak Co., ex-collection Gabriel Cromer
79:0038:28

113
A. COLLARD
French, before 1840-after 1887
Roundhouse for 32 Locomotives at Nevers. Third Interior View
1860-63
Albumen print
From: *Chemin de fer du Bourbonnais*, n.p., ca. 1860-63, pl. 30.
30.7 x 22.0 cm.
Gift of Eastman Kodak Co., ex-collection Gabriel Cromer
79:0038:30

114
PIALLAT
French, active 1860s
Warehouse of Edmond Ganneron, Specialist in Agricultural Equipment
ca. 1865-70
Photolithographic print, plate by Rodier, printed by Bertauts
35.4 x 46.2 cm. (rounded corners)
Museum collection
77:0033:15

115
HYACINTHE CESAR or CLEMENCE JACOB DELMAET and LOUIS-EMILE DURANDELLE
French team, active 1860s-80s
Interior View of the Construction of Ch. Garnier's Opera House
ca. 1864-68
Albumen print
28.0 x 38.6 cm.
Gift of Eastman Kodak Co., ex-collection Gabriel Cromer
80:0099:18

116
HYACINTHE CESAR or CLEMENCE JACOB DELMAET and LOUIS-EMILE DURANDELLE
French team, active 1860s-80s
View of the Roofs of Ch. Garnier's Opera House Under Construction
ca. 1864-68
Albumen print
28.1 x 39.3 cm.
Gift of Eastman Kodak Co., ex-collection Gabriel Cromer
80:0099:10

117
LOUIS-EMILE DURANDELLE
French, active 1860s-80s
Sleeved Industrial Ovens
ca. 1875-80
Albumen print
From: *Eschger Ghesquière & Cie. Fondaries & Laminoirs de Biache St. Vaast (Pas-de-Calais)*
44.2 x 54.1 cm.
Museum purchase
78:0693:3

118
CENTENNIAL PHOTOGRAPHIC COMPANY
American firm, active 1870s
Machinery Hall, North Ave., Looking East (Centennial Exposition)
1876
Albumen print
20.9 x 25.3 cm.
Gift of 3M Company, ex-collection Louis Walton Sipley
77:0372:16

119
FISCHER & BROTHERS
American, active 1850s, 1860s
Gas and Steam Works, U.S. Naval Academy
ca. 1860
Albumen print
15.3 x 20.4 cm. (rounded corners)
Gift of Alden Scott Boyer
80:0273:3

120
UNIDENTIFIED PHOTOGRAPHER
American
Construction Stages of Storage Tank
a. Nov. 21, 1891
b. Dec. 5, 1891
c. Dec. 12, 1891
Gelatin silver prints (3)
18.9 x 24.5; 23.9 x 19.4; and 23.9 x 19.3 cm.
Museum collection
69:0128:1, 2, 3

VI. OLD CITIES AND NEW

121
(NOEL-MARIE PAYMAL LEREBOURS)
French, 1807-73
Le Pont Neuf, View Taken from Lerebours Opticians
1839
Lithographic print, drawn by L. Marquier from a daguerreotype
From: *Daguerréo-Lithographe*, 1839
11.2 x 15.9 cm.
Museum collection
78:0607:4

122
ROBERT MACPHERSON
Scottish, 1811-72
Etruscan Gateway at Perugia
ca. 1858
Albumen print
26.0 x 40.0 cm.
Museum purchase
76:0020:52

123
FR. ALPH. FORTIER
French, died 1882
View Taken from the Pont Notre-Dame, Paris
1853
Salted paper print
From: L.-D. Blanquart-Evrard, *Souvenirs Photographiques*, Lille, ca. 1853.
18.5 x 24.6 cm.
Gift of Alden Scott Boyer
81:1107:3

124
(GIACOMO CANEVA)
Italian, active 1840s-60s
Ruined Bridge on the Tiber
ca. 1850-55
Salted paper print
17.5 x 27.1 cm.
Museum collection
79:1998:2

125
UNIDENTIFIED PHOTOGRAPHER
French
View of the Chateau at Laval from across the Mayenne River
1860
Albumen print
21.2 x 33.0 cm. (domed top)
Gift of Eastman Kodak Co., ex-collection Gabriel Cromer
86:0042:1

126
J. F. MICHIELS
German, active 1850s
Lateral View of the Franc de Bruges Taken from the Pont du Moulin
ca. 1853
Salted paper print
From: L.-D. Blanquart-Evrard, *Variétés photographiques*, Lille, 1853-54.
22.8 x 30.2 cm.
Gift of Eastman Kodak Co., ex-collection Gabriel Cromer
81:1640:1

127
LEOPOLDO, ROMUALDO, and GIUSEPPE ALINARI
Italian, L.: 1832-65; R.: 1830-91; G.: 1836-91
Florence: View of the Arno
ca. 1854-65
Albumen print
32.5 x 24.2 cm.
Museum purchase
76:0332:1

128
UNIDENTIFIED PHOTOGRAPHER
Italian or French
Panorama of Rome
ca. 1850
Salted paper prints (2 attached together)
20.9 x 51.8 (ensemble)
Gift of Alden Scott Boyer
82:1640:1

129
LALA DEEN DAYAL (RAJA)
Indian, 1844-1910
Model of the Residency During the Siege of 1857—Lucknow
1898
Albumen print
19.1 x 26.6 cm.
Gift of the University of Rochester
82:2736:28

130
UNIDENTIFIED PHOTOGRAPHER
Russian or French
Moscow, View of the Kremlin
ca. 1855
Albumen print
20.4 x 25.7 cm.
Museum collection by exchange
74:0184:8

131
GEORGE READ
American, active 1840s
Philadelphia, 3rd and Chestnut Streets
1842
Daguerreotype
Quarter plate, trimmed
Museum purchase
69:0200:41

132
FREDERICK COOMBS
American, active 1840s
Montgomery Street, San Francisco
ca. 1849
Daguerreotype
Half plate
Museum purchase
79:3145:2

133
DR. THOMAS KEITH
Scottish, 1827-95
The High Street, With John Knox's House, Edinburgh
ca. 1855/ca. 1915
Platinum print, printed by Alvin Langdon Coburn
23.9 x 27.0 cm.
Gift of Alvin Langdon Coburn
67:0086:78

134
(LOUIS-DESIRE BLANQUART-EVRARD)
French, 1802-72
Frame House Occupied by Mr. Letriguilly's Bookstore, St. Lô
ca. 1855
Albumen print
From: *Cahier 2*
26.8 x 20.4 cm.
Gift of Kodak Pathé, Vincennes, via the Société française de photographie, ex-collection Henri Fontan
81:1112:2

135
GUILLAUME CLAINE
Belgian, 1811-69
Corporate Houses on the Grand Place, Brussels
ca. 1853
Salted paper print
From: L.-D. Blanquart-Evrard, *Bruxelles photographique*, Lille, ca. 1854.
31.9 x 45.3 cm.
Gift of Eastman Kodak Co., ex-collection Gabriel Cromer
81:1101:3

136
JOSIAH JOHNSON HAWES
American, 1808-1901
Boston Conservatory of Music, Mason Brothers, Publishers, Mason & Hamlin Organ Co., Carriages
ca. 1865
Albumen print
55.7 x 45.4 cm.
Museum purchase
81:1541:2

137
E. & H. T. ANTHONY
American, firm established 1859
a. *Looking Up Broadway from the Corner of Canal Street*
b. *Looking Down Broadway from the Corner of Canal Street*
c. *Broadway on a Rainy Day*
d. *The Broadway Bridge, Including St. Paul's Church and the Astor House*
ca. 1865-68
Albumen prints
Stereographic cards
Gift of Beaumont Newhall (a.); Gifts of Eastman Kodak Co. (b.-d.)
81:8932:12; 81:8932:8; 81:8932:23; 81:8883:1

138
JAMES VALENTINE AND SONS
Scottish, firm established 1880
Cheapside, London
ca. 1885
Albumen print
18.7 x 29.0 cm.
Gift of Alden Scott Boyer
81:2099:4

139
THOMAS ANNAN
Scottish, 1829-87
Old Building, High Street
1868-77
Carbon print
From: *Photographs of the Old Closes, Streets, Etc., Taken 1868-77*, Glasgow, 1878, pl. 16.
26.6 x 34.5 cm.
Museum purchase
75:0054:16

140
THOMAS ANNAN
Scottish, 1829-87
Close No. 61, Saltmarket
1868-77
Carbon print
From: *Photographs of the Old Closes, Streets, Etc., Taken 1868-77*, Glasgow, 1878, pl. 29.
26.7 x 22.2 cm.
Museum purchase
75:0054:29

141
UNIDENTIFIED PHOTOGRAPHER
German
Dovenfleth from the Center End, Hamburg (Free Port)
ca. 1890
Albumen print
32.5 x 24.2 cm.
Museum purchase
77:0617:1

142
HENRY DIXON
British, 1821-1916
Great Saint Helen's, London
1882
Carbon print
From: Society for Photographing Relics of Old London, *Photographing Relics of Old London*, London, 1886, pl. 111.
22.9 x 17.6 cm.
Museum purchase
76:0048:111

143
UNIDENTIFIED PHOTOGRAPHER
German
Dutch District, Hamburg (Free Port)
ca. 1890
Albumen print
24.4 x 33.0 cm.
Museum purchase
77:0617:3

144
UNIDENTIFIED PHOTOGRAPHER
German
Hamburg, View from the Elbe
ca. 1890
Albumen print
24.3 x 22.9 cm.
Museum purchase
77:0617:2

145
WILLIAM H. RAU
American, 1855-1920
Mahanoy City, L.V.R.R.
1899
Albumen print
42.7 x 52.3 cm.
Museum collection
86:0062:1

146
A. C. CHAMPAGNE
French, active 1880s, 1890s
Perspective Along the rue de Castiglione, Panorama of Paris (120°). N. D. Phot. Moëssard Panoramic Camera. Perspective Along the rue de Rivoli.
ca. 1890
Albumen print
20.8 x 54.9 cm.
Gift of Eastman Kodak Co., ex-collection Gabriel Cromer
71:0095:2

147
DR. THOMAS KEITH
Scottish, 1827-95
Edinburgh Castle
ca. 1855/1915
Platinum print, printed by Alvin Langdon Coburn
27.1 x 24.1 cm.
Gift of Alvin Langdon Coburn
67:0086:29

148
FREDERICK H. EVANS
British, 1853-1943
Lincoln Cathedral from the Castle
1898
Platinum print
23.8 x 18.8 cm.
Museum purchase
81:1198:100

149
ALFRED STIEGLITZ
American, 1864-1946
Reflections: Night—New York
1897
Photogravure print
From: A. Stieglitz, *Picturesque Bits of New York and Other Studies*, New York, 1897
12.1 x 23.4 cm.
Museum collection
74:0054:7

CHECKLIST OF WORKS SHOWN AT GEORGE EASTMAN HOUSE ONLY

The following works supplement the exhibition. For reasons of their sizes, formats, or extreme fragility, or for their exclusively local interest, they have been restricted from traveling to other locations. Not illustrated.

I. ANTIQUITY AND ARCHAEOLOGY

I
G. NINCI e CI.
Italian firm, active 1860s
Roman Forum
ca. 1867
Albumen print
60.4 x 153.4 cm.
Museum purchase
76:0207:2

II
KIVORCH and WICHEN ABDULLAH
Turkish team (Abdullah frères), active 1860s
Corridor Adjoining the Kerkhai-Sherif (The Old Seraglio)
1869
Albumen print
From: *Constantinople ancienne & moderne photographiée par Abdullah frères, photographes de S. M. I. le Sultan*, Constantinople, 1869.
22.7 x 30.0 cm.
Museum purchase
77:0005:84

III
TIMOTHY O'SULLIVAN
American, 1840-82
Ancient Ruins in the Canyon de Chelle, N. M. In a Niche 50 Feet Above Present Canyon Bed
1873
Albumen print
From: *Photographs Showing Landscapes, Geological and other Features, of Portions of the Western Territory of the United States, Obtained in Connection with Geographical and Geological Explorations and Surveys West of the 100th Meridian, 1st Lieut. Geo. M. Wheeler, Corps of Engineers, U.S. Army, In Charge*, Washington D. C., 1874-75.
27.3 x 20.4 cm.
Museum purchase
79:0014:41

II. EUROPEAN HISTORY

IV
FRANCIS BEDFORD
British, 1816-94
The Baptistery, Canterbury Cathedral
1859
Albumen print
From: P. H. Delamotte, *The Sunbeam: A Book of Photographs from Nature*, London, 1859, pl. 2
23.4 x 18.2 cm.
Museum collection
86:0059:2

V
JULES ROBUCHON
French, active 1890s
Amailloux (Deux-Sèvres) Chateau de Tennesue
ca. 1890
Carbon print, printed by Dujardin
From: J. Robuchon, *Paysages et Monuments du Poitou*, Paris, 1890, pl. 15
15.9 x 21.5 cm.
Gift of Eastman Kodak Co., ex-collection Gabriel Cromer
86:0060:15

VI
THOMAS ANNAN
Scottish, 1829-87
Mountblow
1870
Carbon print
From: T. Annan, *The Old Country Houses of the Old Glasgow Gentry*, Glasgow, 1870, pl. 75
11.8 x 16.8 cm.
Museum purchase
75:0055:75

VII
BARON JEAN-BAPTISTE-LOUIS GROS
French, 1793-1871
View of the Seine
ca. 1851
Daguerreotype
Full plate
Gift of Eastman Kodak Co., ex-collection Gabriel Cromer
76:0168:135

III. CONTEMPORARY ARCHITECTURAL EXPRESSIONS

VIII
LOUIS-AUGUSTE and AUGUSTE-ROSALIE BISSON
French, L.-A.: 1814-76: A.-R.: 1826-1900
General View of the Chateau Hermières
1858
Albumen print
From: "Presentation Album to Monsieur le Comte F. Baciocchi," Paris, 1858, pl. 11.
31.0 x 41.6 cm.
Museum purchase
77:0405:11

IX
ISAIAH WEST TABER
American, 1830-1912
Baldwin Hotel
ca. 1882
Albumen print
From: I. W. Taber, *View Album and Business Guide, of San Francisco, Photographically Illustrated*, San Francisco, n.d. (ca. 1882), folio 11r.
25.3 x 20.7 cm.
Museum purchase
76:0320:12

IV. THE RUSTIC AND THE VERNACULAR

X
UNIDENTIFIED PHOTOGRAPHER
American
Hancock House, Boston
1853
Salted paper print
From: *Homes of American Statesmen*, New York, 1854, frontispiece
9.6 x 12.5 cm.
Museum purchase

XI
J. A. WHIPPLE
American, 1822-91
Washington's Head-Quarters, Cambridge, Mass.
1855
Crystalotype print
From: *The Photographic & Fine Art Journal*, 1855, pl. 2.
18.5 x 23.5 cm.
Museum collection
86:0058:2

XII
A. A. TURNER
American, active 1860s
Residence of Thomas Cochran, Dobbs Ferry
1860
Photolithographic print
From: *Villas on the Hudson, A Collection of Photo-lithographs of Thirty-one Country Residences*, New York, 1860, pl. 8.
23.6 x 36.0 cm.
Museum purchase
85:1418:8

XIII
ROBERT NEWELL & SON
American, firm active 1870s-
Pump House and Carriage House
ca. 1870s
Albumen print
From: "Artistic Photography," Philadelphia, n.d., pl. 13.
25.9 x 33.9 cm.
Gift of 3M Co., ex-collection Louis Walton Sipley
77:0579:13

XIV
UNIDENTIFIED PHOTOGRAPHER
American
H. H. Warner House, Rochester, New York
ca. 1890
Albumen print
28.0 x 18.3 cm.
Gift of Ms. Edna Kitchner
83:0085:1

V. CONSTRUCTION AND PROGRESS

XV
EDOUARD-DENIS BALDUS
French, 1815-82
Toulon
ca. 1855
Albumen print
From: *Chemins de fer de Paris à Lyon et à la Méditerannée*, Paris, 1855, pl. 71.
27.6 x 43.5 cm.
Museum purchase
74:0055:71

XVI
UNIDENTIFIED PHOTOGRAPHER
French
Cordouan Lighthouse
ca. 1883
Collotype print
From: Léonce Reynaud (ed.) *Les Travaux publics de la France*, vol. 5, (E. Allard, *Phares et Balises*), Paris, 1883, pl. 40
32.1 x 22.1
Museum purchase
78:0800:40, 78:0112:40

VI. OLD CITIES AND NEW

XVIIa
(CLAUDE-HILAIRE-ALPHONSE CHAMOUIN)
French, born 1808
General View of the Quai d'Orsay, Taken with a Daguerreotype
ca. 1850
Drypoint tracing on transparent vellum from a daguerreotype
17.9 x 24.6 cm. (irregular)
Gift of Eastman Kodak Co., ex-collection Gabriel Cromer
80:0218:1

XVIIb
(CLAUDE-HILAIRE-ALPHONSE CHAMOUIN)
French, born 1808
General View of the Quai d'Orsay, Taken with a Daguerreotype
ca. 1850
Steel plate engraving from tracing made from daguerreotype
From: *Collection de vues de Paris prises au daguerréotype*, various editions, ca. 1850-55 (1860), pl. 14
15.7 x 23.2 cm.
Gift of Eastman Kodak Co., ex-collection Gabriel Cromer
75:0151:14

XVIII
EDWARD TOMPKINS WHITNEY
American, born 1820
Corner of State and Main Streets, Rochester, New York
ca. 1852
Daguerreotype
Whole plate
Museum purchase
79:3275:1

XIX
EDOUARD-DENIS BALDUS
French, 1815-82
St. Eustache, Paris
ca. 1856
Albumen print
From: album, *Paris*, Paris, ca. 1858, pl. 13
41.1 x 34.2 cm.
Museum purchase
74:0058:13

XX
GEORGE ROBINSON FARDON
American, active 1850s-60s
St. Francis' Hook and Ladder No. 1. and *Knickerbocker Engine House No. 5.*
ca. 1856
Salted paper prints
From: G. R. Fardon, *San Francisco Album. Photographs of the Most Beautiful Views and Public Buildings of San Francisco*, San Francisco, n.d. (ca. 1856), pl. 12
18.6 x 9.0 and 18.6 x 9.1 cm.
Gift of Eastman Kodak Co., ex-collection Gabriel Cromer
86:0057:13, 14

XXI
MCGLASHAN
Scottish, active 1850s
Bullock Waggon, Melbourn
1856
Albumenized salted paper print
From: T. B. Johnston, *Photographs*, Edinburgh, 1850s, folio 162r
16.1 x 20.5 cm.
Gift of Mr. G. C. Monkhouse
76:0288:163

INDEX TO PHOTOGRAPHERS

SELECTED BIBLIOGRAPHY

This bibliography is intended as a brief guide to the most general and most recent literature on architectural photography, especially that of the last century. Those entries marked by an asterisk(*) contain more extensive bibliographies on the subject.

Basilico, Gabriele, Gaddo Morpurgo, and Italo Zannier (eds.). *Fotografia e immagine dell 'architettura.* Bologna (Comune di Bologna/Galleria d'Arte Moderna), 1980.

Bramson, Henrik, Marianne Brøns, and Bjørn Ochsner. *Early Photographs of Architecture and Views in Two Copenhagen Libraries.* Copenhagen (Thaning and Appel), 1957.

Brown, J. T. "On the Application of Photography to Art and Art Purposes, but more Particularly to Architecture." *The Photographic and Fine Art Journal.* XI, 5 (May 1858), pp. 129-134.

Calvenzi, Giovanna and Gaddo Morpurgo (eds.). *Fotografie di architettura /Photographs of Architecture. Rassegna,* 20, 1979. (*)

Cecchi, Raffaello (ed.). *Lo spazio rubato: architettura e fotografia.* Milan (Edizioni Unicopli), 1983.

Chevrier, Jean-François. "Le dessin photographique." In *L'Architecture en représentation.* Ed. by Gerard Baptiste and Jean-Paul Saint-Aubin. Paris (Inventaire général des monuments et des richesses artistiques de la France), 1985, pp. 188-190.

De Maré, Eric S. *Photography and Architecture.* London (Architectural Press), 1961.

Elwall, Robert. "'The foe-to-graphic art': the rise and fall of the Architectural Photographic Association." *The Photographic Collector.* V, 2 (1985), pp. 142-163.

Gernsheim, Helmut. *Focus on Architecture and Sculpture.* London (The Fountain Press), 1949.

Grefe, Uta. *Die Geschichte der Architekturfotografie des 19. Jahrhunderts: Architekturfotografie—Architekturmalerei.* Unpublished dissertation. Cologne (Universität zu Köln), 1980. (*)

Hales, Peter Bacon. *Silver Cities: The Photography of American Urbanization, 1839-1915.* Philadelphia (Temple University Press), 1984.

Miccini, Eugenio. *Retorica della fotografia, semiotica dell 'architettura rappresentata.* Florence (Alinea Editrice), 1984.

Morrione, Gabriele. *Fotografare l'architettura.* Rome (Edizioni Kappa), 1984.

Néagu, Philippe (ed.). *La Mission héliographique: Photographies de 1851.* Paris (Caisse nationale des monuments historiques et des sites), 1980.

Néagu, Philippe and Jean-François Chevrier. "La Photographie d'architecture aux XIXe et XXe siècles." In *Images et imaginaires d'architecture.* Ed. by Jean Dethier. Paris (Centre national d'art et de culture Georges Pompidou), 1984, pp. 93-101 and *passim.*

Pare, Richard (ed.). *Photography and Architecture: 1839-1939.* Montreal (Centre Canadien d'Architecture), 1982. (*)

Robinson, Cervin and Joel Herschman. *Architecture Transformed: A History of the Photography of Buildings from 1839 to the Present.* Cambridge (M.I.T. Press), forthcoming.

Shulman, Julius. *The Photography of Architecture and Design.* New York (Whitney Architectural Press), 1977.

ACKNOWLEDGEMENTS

As with any project of this scope and size, there are many individuals who have contributed to its realization. Whatever the success of this project, it is in large part due to them; whatever the faults, these can only be mine.

Of the staff of this Museum, particular thanks are due to the two curatorial assistants in my department, Heather Alberts and Joanne Lukitsh, as well as to David Wooters and Carolee Aber of the Print Archives. Rachel Stuhlman, Barbara K. Schaefer, and Rebecca Simmons of the Library aided greatly in my researches; Del Zogg and Sara Beckner of Cataloguing Department brought my attention to details that had otherwise escaped me. Rick Hock, James Via, and Carolyn Zaft of the Exhibitions Department saw the finished exhibition through to its public appearance in their customarily thorough manner. Others on the staff, Ann McCabe and James Conlin of Registration, Marian Early of Print Services, Grant Romer of Conservation, Susan Kramarsky of Marketing Services, Barbara Hall of Publicity, Margorie Grinols of Membership, and Kathleen Wolkowicz of Education are also to be thanked. From the beginning of the project, the Museum's Director, Robert A. Mayer, has been continually supportive and understanding.

In addition, I would like to extend my gratitude to Ms. Jean France and Ms. Deborah Norden for their faith in this endeavor, their trust in my abilities, and their belief in the richness of the collection from which the exhibition was drawn.

The Museum would like to especially thank the Architecture, Planning and Design Program of the New York State Council on the Arts as well as the National Endowment for the Arts, a Federal agency, for their support of this project.

R.A.S.